The Hudson Book of Poetry

150 POEMS WORTH READING

Boston   Burr Ridge, IL   Dubuque, IA   Madison, WI   New York
San Francisco   St. Louis   Bangkok   Bogotá   Caracas   Kuala Lumpur
Lisbon   London   Madrid   Mexico City   Milan   Montreal   New Delhi
Santiago   Seoul   Singapore   Sydney   Taipei   Toronto

McGraw-Hill Higher Education ℞

A Division of The McGraw-Hill Companies

THE HUDSON BOOK OF POETRY: 150 POEMS WORTH READING
Published by McGraw-Hill, an imprint of The McGraw-Hill Companies, Inc. 1221 Avenue of the Americas, New York, NY, 10020. Copyright © 2002, by The McGraw-Hill Companies, Inc. All rights reserved. No part of this publication may be reproduced or distributed in any form or by any means, or stored in a database or retrieval system, without the prior written consent of The McGraw-Hill Companies, Inc., including, but not limited to, in any network or other electronic storage or transmission, or broadcast for distance learning.
Some ancillaries, including electronic and print components, may not be available to customers outside the United States.

This book is printed on acid-free paper.

9 0 DOC/DOC 3

ISBN: 978-0-07-248442-7
MHID: 0-07-248442-X

Director and Publisher: *Phillip A. Butcher*
Senior sponsoring editor: *Sarah Touborg*
Series editor: *Alexis Walker*
Editorial assistant: *Anne Stameshkin*
Senior marketing manager: *David S. Patterson*
Project editor: *Dave Munger*
Website design and development: *The Davidson Group*
Project manager: *Laura Ward Majersky*
Production supervisor: *Gina Hangos*
New media producer: *Gregg DiLorenzo*
Cover design: *Artemio Ortiz Jr.*
Cover image: *V. De Grailly, West Point. Courtesy of Fruitlands Museums, Harvard, MA*
Printer: *R.R. Donnelley & Sons Company*
Typeface: *9.5/11 Sabon*
Compositor: *Carlisle Communications, Ltd.*

Library of Congress Control Number: 2001087945

www.mhhe.com

Table of Contents

Preface

> *If you would not be forgotten, as soon as*
> *you are dead & rotten, either write things*
> *worth reading, or do things worth the writing.*
> —Benjamin Franklin

Good literature is worth reading. This might seem obvious, but given all the competition for our time in these increasingly wired and global days, it bears repeating. Reading allows you to dream strange dreams, to live out bold adventures, and to see the world around you in utterly new ways—all at your own pace, and even (if necessary) during a power failure.

This text is an attempt to make those important experiences a bit easier for all of us. Stripped bare of the kind of apparatus that can obscure the forest with too many trees, made as inexpensive as possible while still remaining publishable, and containing 150 poems truly worth the trouble, *The Hudson Book of Poetry* offers an alternative to textbooks that look like phonebooks (and cost a whole lot more).

The Hudson Book of Poetry in Print

We've put together the following in the print version of this text:

- 150 poems with their dates of publication°
- biographical information on the authors
- a timeline linking the texts to historical context

In most cases, we provide the date of first publication. Parentheses indicate dates of composition.

The Hudson Book of Poetry Online

For those of you at home in the wired world, we've also put the complete text of 69 of the poems online at www.mhhe.com/hudson150, with hyperlinks to an online dictionary and to relevant sites that literally put pictures to words. (Texts available online are marked with the ◨ icon.) Also online, for those who want them, are questions geared to specific poems and accompanying writing suggestions.

We'd like to thank the following instructors for telling us which poems they think their students can't do without:

Jacqueline Agesilas, Antillean Adventist University
Robert G. Blake, Elon College
Anthony Boyle, SUNY Potsdam
Alan Brown, University of West Alabama
Alan Chavkin, Southwest Texas State University
Nancy Chavkin, Southwest Texas State University
Andrea DeFusco, Boston College
Anneliese Eckhardt, Guilford Technical Community College
Carol B. Gartner, Purdue University—Calumet
Matthew K. Gold, CUNY Graduate Center
Anthony Hunt, University of Puerto Rico—Mayagüez
Sherrie Inness, Miami University
Philip K. Jason, United States Naval Academy
Beth Kemper, Campbellsville University
Thomas M. Kitts, St. John's University
David Mason, Colorado College
Nancy McCabe, Presbyterian College
Robert S. Newman, SUNY Buffalo
Kathleen C. Peirce, Southwest Texas State University
Cecilia Ready, Villanova University
Diana Royer, Miami University
Angela Salas, Adrian College
James W. Stick, Jr., Des Moines Area Community College

For additional help in the preparation of this book, huge thanks go to: Dave Munger; The Davidson Group; Chrysta Meadowbrooke; Dianne Hall; Sarah Touborg, Anne Stameshkin, Lisa Moore, Chris Narozny, Victoria Fullard, Carla Samodulski, Phil Butcher, Ray Kelley, and David S. Patterson of the English team at McGraw-Hill; Laura Majersky and Artemio Ortiz; Michael Volmar of Fruitlands Museums; Tom Kitts; Warren Habib; and Claudia Walker Habib.

Note to students: Turn the page and start reading. With any luck, you'll find yourself hooked.

Anonymous

WESTERN WIND 🎵

(English lyric)

Western wind, when will thou blow,
    The small rain down can rain?
Christ! if my love were in my arms
    And I in my bed again!

(ca. 1500)

SIR PATRICK SPENCE 🎵

(traditional Scottish ballad)

The king sits in Dumferling toune,
    Drinking the blude-reid wine:
"O whar will I get guid sailor,
    To sail this schip of mine?"

Up and spak an eldern knicht,   5
    Sat at the kings richt kne:
"Sir Patrick Spence is the best sailor
    That sails upon the se."

The king has written a braid letter,
    And signed it wi' his hand,   10
And sent it to Sir Patrick Spence,
    Was walking on the sand.

The first line that Sir Patrick red,
    A loud lauch lauchèd he;
The next line that Sir Patrick red,   15
    The teir blinded his ee.

"O wha° is this has don this deid,
    This ill deid don to me,
To send me out this time o' the yeir,
    To sail upon the se!   20

_____

17 wha who

"Mak haste, mak haste, my mirry men all,
   Our guid schip sails the morne."
"O say na sae,° my master deir,
   For I feir a deadlie storme.

"Late late yestreen I saw the new moone,   25
   Wi' the auld moone in hir arme,
And I feir, I feir, my deir master,
   That we will cum to harme."

O our Scots nobles wer richt laith°
   To weet° their cork-heiled schoone,°   30
Bot lang owre° a' the play wer playd,
   Their hats they swam aboone.°

O lang, lang may their ladies sit,
   Wi' their fans into their hand,
Or ere they se Sir Patrick Spence   35
   Cum sailing to the land.

O lang, lang may the ladies stand,
   Wi' their gold kems° in their hair,
Waiting for their ain° deir lords,
   For they'll se thame na mair.   40

Haf owre,° haf owre to Aberdour
   It's fiftie fadom deip,
And thair lies guid Sir Patrick Spence,
   Wi' the Scots lords at his feit.

---

23 **sae** so   **29 laith** loath   **30 weet** wet   **schoone** shoes   **31 owre** before
32 aboone above   **38 kems** combs   **39 ain** own   **41 Haf owre** halfway over

Sir Walter Raleigh
ca. 1552–1618

THE NYMPH'S REPLY 🄝

If all the world and love were young,
And truth in every shepherd's tongue,
These pretty pleasures might me move
To live with thee and be thy love.

Time drives the flocks from field to fold,   5
When rivers rage and rocks grow cold,
And Philomel° becometh dumb;
The rest complains of cares to come.

The flowers do fade, and wanton fields
To wayward winter reckoning yields;   10
A honey tongue, a heart of gall,
Is fancy's spring, but sorrow's fall.

Thy gowns, thy shoes, thy beds of roses,
Thy cap, thy kirtle,° and thy posies
Soon break, soon wither, soon forgotten,—   15
In folly ripe, in reason rotten.

Thy belt of straw and ivy buds,
The coral clasps and amber studs,
All these in me no means can move
To come to thee and be thy love.   20

But could youth last and love still breed,
Had joys no date nor age no need,
Then these delights my mind might move
To live with thee and be thy love.

    —1600

---

7 Philomel the nightingale   **14 kirtle** skirt

Michael Drayton
1563–1631

SINCE THERE'S NO HELP ♫

Since there's no help, come let us kiss and part;
Nay, I have done, you get no more of me,
And I am glad, yea, glad with all my heart
That thus so cleanly I myself can free;
Shake hands for ever, cancel all our vows,   5
And when we meet at any time again,
Be it not seen in either of our brows
That we one jot of former love retain.
Now at the last gasp of Love's latest breath,
When, his pulse failing, Passion speechless lies,   10
When Faith is kneeling by his bed of death,
And Innocence is closing up his eyes,
        Now if thou wouldst, when all have given him over,
        From death to life thou mightst him yet recover.

        —1619

Christopher Marlowe
1564–1593

THE PASSIONATE SHEPHERD TO HIS LOVE ♫

Come live with me and be my love,
And we will all the pleasures prove
That valleys, groves, hills, and fields,
Woods, or steepy mountain yields.

And we will sit upon the rocks,   5
Seeing the shepherds feed their flocks

By shallow rivers, to whose falls
Melodious birds sing madrigals.

And I will make thee beds of roses
And a thousand fragrant posies,   10
A cap of flowers and a kirtle°
Embroidered all with leaves of myrtle;

A gown made of the finest wool
Which from our pretty lambs we pull;
Fair-linèd slippers for the cold,   15
With buckles of the purest gold;

A belt of straw and ivy buds,
With coral clasps and amber studs.
And if these pleasures may thee move,
Come live with me and be my love.   20

The shepherds' swains shall dance and sing
For thy delight each May morning.
If these delights thy mind may move,
Then live with me and be my love.

    —1599

William Shakespeare
1564–1616

SONNET 18 🔊

Shall I compare thee to a summer's day?
Thou art more lovely and more temperate:
Rough winds do shake the darling buds of May,
And summer's lease hath all too short a date:
Sometimes too hot the eye of heaven shines,   5
And often is his gold complexion dimmed;

---

11 kirtle skirt

And every fair° from fair sometimes declines,
By chance or nature's changing course untrimmed;
But thy eternal summer shall not fade,
Nor lose possession of that fair thou ow'st;°   10
Nor shall death brag thou wander'st in his shade,
When in eternal lines to time thou grow'st:
So long as men can breathe, or eyes can see,
So long lives this, and this gives life to thee.

    —1609

SONNET 29 🔊

When, in disgrace with fortune and men's eyes,
I all alone beweep my outcast state,
And trouble deaf heaven with my bootless cries,
And look upon myself, and curse my fate,
Wishing me like to one more rich in hope,   5
Featured like him, like him with friends possessed,
Desiring this man's art and that man's scope,
With what I most enjoy contented least;
Yet in these thoughts myself almost despising,
Haply I think on thee—and then my state,   10
Like to the lark at break of day arising
From sullen earth, sings hymns at heaven's gate;
For thy sweet love remembered such wealth brings
That then I scorn to change my state with kings.

    —1609

SONNET 73 🔊

That time of year thou mayst in me behold
When yellow leaves, or none, or few, do hang
Upon those boughs which shake against the cold,
Bare ruined choirs, where late the sweet birds sang.
In me thou see'st the twilight of such day   5
As after sunset fadeth in the west;
Which by and by black night doth take away,
Death's second self, that seals up all in rest.

---

7 **fair** fair thing   10 **ow'st** ownest

In me thou see'st the glowing of such fire,
That on the ashes of his youth doth lie,   10
As the deathbed whereon it must expire,
Consumed with that which it was nourished by.
This thou perceiv'st, which makes thy love more strong,
To love that well which thou must leave ere long.

—1609

SONNET 130 🔊

My mistress' eyes are nothing like the sun;
Coral is far more red than her lips' red;
If snow be white, why then her breasts are dun;
If hairs be wires, black wires grow on her head.
I have seen roses damasked, red and white,   5
But no such roses see I in her cheeks;
And in some perfumes is there more delight
Than in the breath that from my mistress reeks.
I love to hear her speak, yet well I know
That music hath a far more pleasing sound;   10
I grant I never saw a goddess go;
My mistress, when she walks, treads on the ground.
And yet, by heaven, I think my love as rare
As any she° belied° with false compare.°

—1609

---

14 she woman   **belied** lied about   **compare** comparisons

Thomas Campion
1567–1620

THERE IS A GARDEN
IN HER FACE 🎵

There is a garden in her face,
Where roses and white lilies grow,
A heavenly paradise is that place,
Wherein all pleasant fruits do flow.
There cherries grow which none may buy   5
Till "Cherry-ripe!" themselves do cry.

Those cherries fairly do enclose
Of orient pearl a double row,
Which when her lovely laughter shows,
They look like rosebuds filled with snow.   10
Yet them nor peer nor prince can buy,
Till "Cherry-ripe!" themselves do cry.

Her eyes like angels watch them still;
Her brows like bended bows do stand,
Threatening with piercing frowns to kill   15
All that attempt with eye or hand
Those sacred cherries to come nigh,
Till "Cherry-ripe!" themselves do cry.

—1617

John Donne
1572–1631

DEATH BE NOT PROUD 🔊

Death be not proud, though some have callèd thee
Mighty and dreadful, for thou art not so;
For those whom thou think'st thou dost overthrow
Die not, poor death, nor yet canst thou kill me.
From rest and sleep, which but thy pictures be,   5
Much pleasure, then from thee much more must flow,
And soonest our best men with thee do go,
Rest of their bones, and soul's delivery.
Thou art slave to fate, chance, kings, and desperate men,
And dost with poison, war, and sickness dwell,   10
And poppy, or charms can make us sleep as well
And better than thy stroke; why swell'st thou then?
One short sleep past, we wake eternally,
And death shall be no more; death, thou shalt die.

(ca. 1610)

A VALEDICTION: FORBIDDING MOURNING 🔊

As virtuous men pass mildly away,
    And whisper to their souls to go,
Whilst some of their sad friends do say
    The breath goes now, and some say no:

So let us melt, and make no noise,   5
    No tear-floods, nor sigh-tempests move;
'Twere profanation of our joys
    To tell the laity our love.

Moving of th' earth brings harms and fears;
    Men reckon what it did and meant;   10

But trepidation of the spheres,°
   Though greater far, is innocent.

Dull sublunary lovers' love
   (Whose soul is sense) cannot admit
Absence, because it doth remove   15
   Those things which elemented it.

But we, by a love so much refined
   That ourselves know not what it is,
Inter-assurèd of the mind,
   Care less, eyes, lips, and hands to miss.   20

Our two souls, therefore, which are one,
   Though I must go, endure not yet
A breach, but an expansiòn,
   Like gold to airy thinness beat.

If they be two, they are two so   25
   As stiff twin compasses are two:
Thy soul, the fixed foot, makes no show
   To move, but doth, if th' other do.

And though it in the center sit,
   Yet when the other far doth roam,   30
It leans and harkens after it,
   And grows erect as that comes home.

Such wilt thou be to me, who must,
   Like th' other foot, obliquely run;
Thy firmness makes my circle just,   35
   And makes me end where I begun.

     (1611)

---

11 **spheres** heavenly spheres, in Ptolemaic astronomy

SONG 🔃

Go and catch a falling star,
   Get with child a mandrake root,°
Tell me where all past years are,
   Or who cleft the Devil's foot,
Teach me to hear mermaids singing,   5
   Or to keep off envy's stinging,
       And find
       What wind
Serves to advance an honest mind.

If thou be'st borne to strange sights,   10
   Things invisible to see,
Ride ten thousand days and nights,
   Till age snow white hairs on thee,
Thou, when thou return'st, wilt tell me
   All strange wonders that befell thee,   15
       And swear
       Nowhere
Lives a woman true, and fair.

If thou findst one, let me know,
   Such a pilgrimage were sweet—   20
Yet do not, I would not go,
   Though at next door we might meet;
Though she were true, when you met her,
   And last, till you write your letter,
       Yet she   25
       Will be
False, ere I come, to two, or three.

   —1633

---

2 mandrake root The mandrake root is forked and so resembles the lower part of the human body.

Ben Jonson
1 5 7 3 ? – 1 6 3 7

ON MY FIRST SON

Farewell, thou child of my right hand, and joy.
My sin was too much hope of thee, loved boy;
Seven years thou wert lent to me, and I thee pay,
Exacted by thy fate, on the just day.
Oh, could I lose all father now. For why   5
Will man lament the state he should envỳ?—
To have so soon 'scaped world's and flesh's rage,
And, if no other misery, yet age.
Rest in soft peace, and asked, say, "Here doth lie
Ben Jonson his best piece of poetry,"   10
For whose sake henceforth all his vows be such
As what he loves may never like too much.

    (1603)

TO CELIA

Drink to me only with thine eyes,
   And I will pledge with mine;
Or leave a kiss but in the cup,
   And I'll not ask for wine.
The thirst that from the soul doth rise   5
   Doth ask a drink divine;
But might I of Jove's nectar sup,
   I would not change for thine.

I sent thee late a rosy wreath,
   Not so much honoring thee   10
As giving it a hope that there
   It could not withered be.
But thou thereon didst only breathe,
   And sent'st it back to me;
Since when it grows, and smells, I swear,   15
   Not of itself but thee.

    —1616

Robert Herrick
1591–1674

TO THE VIRGINS,
TO MAKE MUCH OF TIME 🔊

Gather ye rosebuds while ye may,
   Old time is still a-flying;
And this same flower that smiles today
   Tomorrow will be dying.

The glorious lamp of heaven, the sun,   5
   The higher he's a-getting,
The sooner will his race be run,
   And nearer he's to setting.

That age is best which is the first,
   When youth and blood are warmer;   10
But being spent, the worse, and worst
   Times still succeed the former.

Then be not coy, but use your time,
   And, while ye may, go marry;
For, having lost but once your prime,   15
   You may forever tarry.

   —1648

George Herbert
1593–1633

EASTER WINGS ◨

Lord, who createdst man in wealth and store,
   Though foolishly he lost the same,
      Decaying more and more
        Till he became
         Most poor: 5
        With Thee
       O let me rise
     As larks, harmoniously,
   And sing this day Thy victories:
Then shall the fall further the flight in me.   10

My tender age in sorrow did begin;
   And still with sicknesses and shame
      Thou didst so punish sin,
        That I became
         Most thin.   15
        With Thee
       Let me combine,
     And feel this day thy victory;
   For, if I imp° my wing on thine,
Affliction shall advance the flight in me.   20

   —1633

----

19 imp graft

John Milton
1608–1674

WHEN I CONSIDER
HOW MY LIGHT IS SPENT ◾

When I consider how my light is spent
   Ere half my days, in this dark world and wide,
   And that one talent which is death to hide°
   Lodged with me useless, though my soul more bent
To serve therewith my Maker, and present   5
   My true account, lest he returning chide;
   "Doth God exact day-labor, light denied?"
   I fondly° ask; but Patience to prevent
That murmur, soon replies, "God doth not need
   Either man's work or his own gifts; who best   10
   Bear his mild yoke, they serve him best. His state
Is kingly. Thousands at his bidding speed
   And post o'er land and ocean without rest:
   They also serve who only stand and wait."

   (1655?)

Anne Bradstreet
1612?–1672

THE AUTHOR TO HER BOOK ◾

Thou ill-formed offspring of my feeble brain,
Who after birth didst by my side remain,
Till snatched from thence by friends, less wise than true,
Who thee abroad, exposed to public view,
Made thee in rags, halting to th' press to trudge,   5

---

3 hide a reference to Matthew 25:14–30   **8 fondly** foolishly

Where errors were not lessened (all may judge).
At thy return my blushing was not small,
My rambling brat (in print) should mother call,
I cast thee by as one unfit for light,
Thy visage was so irksome in my sight;   10
Yet being mine own, at length affection would
Thy blemishes amend, if so I could:
I washed thy face, but more defects I saw,
And rubbing off a spot still made a flaw.
I stretched thy joints to make thee even feet,   15
Yet still thou run'st more hobbling than is meet;
In better dress to trim thee was my mind,
But nought save homespun cloth i' th' house I find.
In this array 'mongst vulgars may'st thou roam.
In critic's hands beware thou dost not come,   20
And take thy way where yet thou art not known;
If for thy father asked, say thou hadst none;
And for thy mother, she alas is poor,
Which caused her thus to send thee out of door.

        —1678

TO MY DEAR AND
LOVING HUSBAND 🔊

If ever two were one, then surely we;
If ever man were loved by wife, then thee;
If ever wife was happy in a man,
Compare with me, ye women, if you can.
I prize thy love more than whole mines of gold,   5
Or all the riches that the East doth hold.
My love is such that rivers cannot quench,
Nor aught but love from thee give recompense.
Thy love is such I can no way repay;
The heavens reward thee manifold, I pray.   10
Then while we live in love let's so persever
That when we live no more we may live ever.

        —1678

Richard Lovelace
1 6 1 8 – 1 6 5 8

TO LUCASTA 🔊

on Going to the Wars

Tell me not, Sweet, I am unkind
    That from the nunnery
Of thy chaste breast and quiet mind,
    To war and arms I fly.

True, a new mistress now I chase,   5
    The first foe in the field;
And with a stronger faith embrace
    A sword, a horse, a shield.

Yet this inconstancy is such
    As you too shall adore;   10
I could not love thee, Dear, so much,
    Loved I not Honor more.

     —1649

Andrew Marvell
1 6 2 1 – 1 6 7 8

TO HIS COY MISTRESS 🔊

    Had we but world enough, and time,
This coyness, lady, were no crime.
We would sit down, and think which way
To walk, and pass our long love's day.
Thou by the Indian Ganges' side   5
Shouldst rubies find; I by the tide

Of Humber° would complain. I would
Love you ten years before the flood,
And you should, if you please, refuse
Till the conversion of the Jews.°   10
My vegetable° love should grow
Vaster than empires, and more slow;
An hundred years should go to praise
Thine eyes, and on thy forehead gaze;
Two hundred to adore each breast,   15
But thirty thousand to the rest;
An age at least to every part,
And the last age should show your heart.
For, lady, you deserve this state,°
Nor would I love at lower rate.   20
    But at my back I always hear
Time's wingèd chariot hurrying near;
And yonder all before us lie
Deserts of vast eternity.
Thy beauty shall no more be found;   25
Nor, in thy marble vault, shall sound
My echoing song; then worms shall try
That long-preserved virginity,
And your quaint honor turn to dust,
And into ashes all my lust: 30
The grave's a fine and private place,
But none, I think, do there embrace.
    Now therefore, while the youthful hue
Sits on thy skin like morning glow,
And while thy willing soul transpires   35
At every pore with instant fires,
Now let us sport us while we may,
And now, like amorous birds of prey,
Rather at once our time devour
Than languish in his slow-chapped° power.   40
Let us roll all our strength and all
Our sweetness up into one ball,
And tear our pleasures with rough strife
Thorough the iron gates of life:
Thus, though we cannot make our sun   45
Stand still, yet we will make him run.

        —1681

---

7 **Humber** an English river   10 **conversion of the Jews** at the end of time
11 **vegetable** flourishing   19 **state** stateliness; pomp   40 **chapped** jawed

Jonathan Swift
1667–1745

A DESCRIPTION
OF THE MORNING 🄰

Now hardly here and there an hackney-coach,
Appearing, showed the ruddy morn's approach.
Now Betty from her master's bed had flown
And softly stole to discompose her own.
The slipshod 'prentice from his master's door   5
Had pared the dirt, and sprinkled round the floor.
Now Moll had whirled her mop with dextrous airs,
Prepared to scrub the entry and the stairs.
The youth with broomy stumps began to trace
The kennel°-edge, where wheels had worn the place.   10
The small-coal man was heard with cadence deep
Till drowned in shriller notes of chimneysweep,
Duns° at his lordship's gate began to meet,
And Brickdust Moll° had screamed through half the street.
The turnkey° now his flock returning sees,   15
Duly let out a-nights to steal for fees;
The watchful bailiffs take their silent stands;
And schoolboys lag with satchels in their hands.

　(1711)

---

10 **kennel** gutter   13 **Duns** bill-collectors   14 **Brickdust Moll** a seller of powdered
brick used for cleaning   15 **turnkey** jailor

Alexander Pope
1688–1744

from AN ESSAY ON CRITICISM 🔊

True ease in writing comes from art, not chance,
As those move easiest who have learned to dance.
'Tis not enough no harshness gives offense,
The sound must seem an echo to the sense.   365
Soft is the strain when Zephyr° gently blows,
And the smooth stream in smoother numbers flows;
But when loud surges lash the sounding shore,
The hoarse, rough verse should like the torrent roar.
When Ajax° strives some rock's vast weight to throw,   370
The line too labors, and the words move slow;
Not so when swift Camilla° scours the plain,
Flies o'er the unbending corn, and skims along the main.
Hear how Timotheus'° varied lays surprise,
And bid alternate passions fall and rise!   375
While at each change the son of Libyan Jove°
Now burns with glory, and then melts with love;
Now his fierce eyes with sparkling fury glow,
Now sighs steal out, and tears begin to flow:
Persians and Greeks like turns of nature found   380
And the world's victor stood subdued by sound!
The power of music all our hearts allow,
And what Timotheus was is Dryden now.
      Avoid extremes; and shun the fault of such
Who still are pleased too little or too much.   385
At every trifle scorn to take offense:
That always shows great pride, or little sense.
Those heads, as stomachs, are not sure the best,
Which nauseate all, and nothing can digest.
Yet let not each gay turn thy rapture move;   390
For fools admire, but men of sense approve:
As things seem large which we through mists descry,
Dullness is ever apt to magnify.

      —1711

---

366 **Zephyr** the west wind   370 **Ajax** Greek hero from the *Iliad*   372 **Camilla** figure
from the *Aeneid* known for speed and grace   374 **Timotheus** a favorite musician of
Alexander the Great   376 **son of Libyan Jove** Alexander the Great

EPIGRAM

Engraved on the Collar of a Dog
Which I Gave to His Royal Highness

I am his Highness' dog at Kew;
Pray tell me, sir, whose dog are you?

—1738

Phillis Wheatley
1 7 5 3 ? – 1 7 8 4

TO THE UNIVERSITY OF CAMBRIDGE, IN NEW-ENGLAND

While an intrinsic ardor prompts to write,
The muses promise to assist my pen;
'Twas not long since I left my native shore
The land of errors, and *Egyptian* gloom:
Father of mercy, 'twas thy gracious hand   5
Brought me in safety from those dark abodes.

    Students, to you 'tis giv'n to scan the heights
Above, to traverse the ethereal space,
And mark the systems of revolving worlds.
Still more, ye sons of science ye receive   10
The blissful news by messengers from heav'n,
How *Jesus'* blood for your redemption flows.
See him with hands out-stretcht upon the cross;
Immense compassion in his bosom glows;
He hears revilers, nor resents their scorn: 15
What matchless mercy in the Son of God!
When the whole human race by sin had fall'n,
He deign'd to die that they might rise again,
And share with him in the sublimest skies,
Life without death, and glory without end.   20

Improve your privileges while they stay,
Ye pupils, and each hour redeem, that bears
Or good or bad report of you to heav'n.
Let sin, that baneful evil to the soul,
By you be shunn'd, nor once remit your guard;　　　　25
Suppress the deadly serpent in its egg.
Ye blooming plants of human race devine,
An *Ethiop* tells you 'tis your greatest foe;
Its transient sweetness turns to endless pain,
And in immense perdition sinks the soul.　　　　30

—1773

William Blake
1757–1827

THE TYGER 🔁

Tyger! Tyger! burning bright
In the forests of the night,
What immortal hand or eye
Could frame thy fearful symmetry?

In what distant deeps or skies　　　　5
Burnt the fire of thine eyes?
On what wings dare he aspire?
What the hand dare seize the fire?

And what shoulder, and what art,
Could twist the sinews of thy heart?　　　　10
And when thy heart began to beat,
What dread hand? and what dread feet?

What the hammer? what the chain?
In what furnace was thy brain?
What the anvil? what dread grasp　　　　15
Dare its deadly terrors clasp?

When the stars threw down their spears,
And watered heaven with their tears,
Did he smile his work to see?
Did he who made the Lamb make thee?   20

Tyger! Tyger! burning bright
In the forests of the night,
What immortal hand or eye,
Dare frame thy fearful symmetry?

   —1794

THE SICK ROSE 🔃

O Rose, thou art sick!
The invisible worm
That flies in the night,
In the howling storm,

Has found out thy bed   5
Of crimson joy,
And his dark secret love
Does thy life destroy.

   —1794

LONDON 🔃

I wander through each chartered street,
Near where the chartered Thames does flow,
And mark in every face I meet
Marks of weakness, marks of woe.

In every cry of every man,   5
In every infant's cry of fear,
In every voice, in every ban,
The mind-forged manacles I hear.

How the chimney-sweeper's cry
Every black'ning church appalls   10
And the hapless soldier's sigh
Runs in blood down palace walls.

But most through midnight streets I hear
How the youthful harlot's curse
Blasts the new born infant's tear   15
And blights with plagues the marriage hearse.

—1794

William Wordsworth
1770–1850

LINES COMPOSED A FEW MILES ABOVE TINTERN ABBEY

on Revisiting the Banks of the Wye During a Tour, July 13, 1798

   Five years have passed; five summers, with the length
Of five long winters! and again I hear
These waters, rolling from their mountain-springs
With a sweet inland murmur.—Once again
Do I behold these steep and lofty cliffs,   5
That on a wild secluded scene impress
Thoughts of more deep seclusion; and connect
The landscape with the quiet of the sky.
The day is come when I again repose
Here, under this dark sycamore, and view   10
These plots of cottage ground, these orchard tufts,
Which at this season, with their unripe fruits,
Are clad in one green hue, and lose themselves
'Mid groves and copses. Once again I see
These hedgerows, hardly hedgerows, little lines   15
Of sportive wood run wild; these pastoral farms,
Green to the very door; and wreaths of smoke
Sent up, in silence, from among the trees!
With some uncertain notice, as might seem
Of vagrant dwellers in the houseless woods,   20
Or of some Hermit's cave, where by his fire
The Hermit sits alone.

These beauteous forms,
Through a long absence, have not been to me
As is a landscape to a blind man's eye;
But oft, in lonely rooms, and 'mid the din   25
Of towns and cities, I have owed to them,
In hours of weariness, sensations sweet,
Felt in the blood, and felt along the heart;
And passing even into my purer mind,
With tranquil restoration:—feelings too   30
Of unremembered pleasure; such, perhaps,
As have no slight or trivial influence
On that best portion of a good man's life,
His little, nameless, unremembered, acts
Of kindness and of love. Nor less, I trust,   35
To them I may have owed another gift,
Of aspect more sublime; that blessed mood,
In which the burthen of the mystery,
In which the heavy and the weary weight
Of all this unintelligible world,   40
Is lightened—that serene and blessed mood,
In which the affections gently lead us on—
Until, the breath of this corporeal frame
And even the motion of our human blood
Almost suspended, we are laid asleep   45
In body, and become a living soul;
While with an eye made quiet by the power
Of harmony, and the deep power of joy,
We see into the life of things.

If this
Be but a vain belief, yet, oh! how oft—   50
In darkness and amid the many shapes
Of joyless daylight; when the fretful stir
Unprofitable, and the fever of the world,
Have hung upon the beatings of my heart—
How oft, in spirit, have I turned to thee,   55
O sylvan Wye! Thou wanderer through the woods,
How often has my spirit turned to thee!

And now, with gleams of half-extinguished thought,
With many recognitions dim and faint,
And somewhat of a sad perplexity,   60
The picture of the mind revives again:
While here I stand, not only with the sense
Of present pleasure, but with pleasing thoughts
That in this moment there is life and food
For future years. And so I dare to hope,   65

Though changed, no doubt, from what I was when first
I came among these hills; when like a roe
I bounded o'er the mountains, by the sides
Of the deep rivers, and the lonely streams,
Wherever nature led—more like a man   70
Flying from something that he dreads than one
Who sought the thing he loved. For nature then
(The coarser pleasures of my boyish days,
And their glad animal movements all gone by)
To me was all in all.—I cannot paint   75
What then I was. The sounding cataract
Haunted me like a passion: the tall rock,
The mountain, and the deep and gloomy wood,
Their colours and their forms, were then to me
An appetite: a feeling and a love,   80
That had no need of a remoter charm,
By thought supplied, or any interest
Unborrowed from the eye.—That time is past,
And all its aching joys are now no more,
And all its dizzy raptures. Not for this   85
Faint I, nor mourn nor murmur: other gifts
Have followed; for such loss, I would believe,
Abundant recompense. For I have learned
To look on nature, not as in the hour
Of thoughtless youth; but hearing oftentimes   90
The still, sad music of humanity,
Nor harsh nor grating, though of ample power
To chasten and subdue. And I have felt
A presence that disturbs me with the joy
Of elevated thoughts; a sense sublime   95
Of something far more deeply interfused,
Whose dwelling is the light of setting suns,
And the round ocean and the living air,
And the blue sky, and in the mind of man:
A motion and a spirit, that impels   100
All thinking things, all objects of all thought,
And rolls through all things. Therefore am I still
A lover of the meadows and the woods,
And mountains; and of all that we behold
From this green earth; of all the mighty world   105
Of eye, and ear—both what they half create,
And what perceive; well pleased to recognize
In nature and the language of the sense
The anchor of my purest thoughts, the nurse,
The guide, the guardian of my heart, and soul   110
Of all my moral being.

                    Nor, perchance,
If I were not thus taught, should I the more
Suffer my genial spirits to decay:
For thou art with me, here, upon the banks
Of this fair river; thou, my dearest Friend,°   115
My dear, dear Friend; and in thy voice I catch
The language of my former heart, and read
My former pleasures in the shooting lights
Of thy wild eyes. Oh! yet a little while
May I behold in thee what I was once,   120
My dear, dear Sister! And this prayer I make,
Knowing that Nature never did betray
The heart that loved her; 'tis her privilege,
Through all the years of this our life, to lead
From joy to joy: for she can so inform   125
The mind that is within us, so impress
With quietness and beauty, and so feed
With lofty thoughts, that neither evil tongues,
Rash judgments, nor the sneers of selfish men,
Nor greetings where no kindness is, nor all   130
The dreary intercourse of daily life,
Shall e'er prevail against us, or disturb
Our cheerful faith, that all which we behold
Is full of blessings. Therefore let the moon
Shine on thee in thy solitary walk;   135
And let the misty mountain winds be free
To blow against thee: and, in after years,
When these wild ecstasies shall be matured
Into a sober pleasure; when thy mind
Shall be a mansion for all lovely forms,   140
Thy memory be as a dwelling place
For all sweet sounds and harmonies; oh! then,
If solitude, or fear, or pain, or grief,
Should be thy portion, with what healing thoughts
Of tender joy wilt thou remember me,   145
And these my exhortations! Nor, perchance—
If I should be, where I no more can hear
Thy voice, nor catch from thy wild eyes these gleams
Of past existence—wilt thou then forget
That on the banks of this delightful stream   150
We stood together; and that I, so long
A worshipper of Nature, hither came,
Unwearied in that service: rather say
With warmer love,—oh! with far deeper zeal

---

115 **Friend** the poet's sister Dorothy (1771–1855)

Of holier love. Nor wilt thou then forget,   155
That after many wanderings, many years
Of absence, these steep woods and lofty cliffs,
And this green pastoral landscape, were to me
More dear, both for themselves and for thy sake!

—1798

COMPOSED UPON WESTMINSTER BRIDGE 𝕟

September 3, 1802

Earth has not anything to show more fair:
Dull would he be of soul who could pass by
A sight so touching in its majesty:
This City now doth, like a garment, wear
The beauty of the morning; silent, bare,   5
Ships, towers, domes, theatres, and temples lie
Open unto the fields, and to the sky;
All bright and glittering in the smokeless air.
Never did sun more beautifully steep
In his first splendor, valley, rock, or hill;   10
Ne'er saw I, never felt, a calm so deep!
The river glideth at his own sweet will:
Dear God! the very houses seem asleep;
And all that mighty heart is lying still!

—1807

THE WORLD IS TOO MUCH WITH US 𝕟

The world is too much with us; late and soon,
Getting and spending, we lay waste our powers;
Little we see in Nature that is ours;
We have given our hearts away, a sordid boon!
This Sea that bares her bosom to the moon;   5
The winds that will be howling at all hours,
And are up-gathered now like sleeping flowers;
For this, for everything, we are out of tune;
It moves us not. Great God! I'd rather be
A Pagan suckled in a creed outworn;   10

So might I, standing on this pleasant lea,
Have glimpses that would make me less forlorn;
Have sight of Proteus rising from the sea;
Or hear old Triton blow his wreathèd horn.

—1807

Samuel Taylor Coleridge
1772–1834

KUBLA KHAN° ▣

Or, a Vision in a Dream. A Fragment.

In Xanadu did Kubla Khan
A stately pleasure-dome decree:
Where Alph, the sacred river, ran
Through caverns measureless to man
   Down to a sunless sea.   5
So twice five miles of fertile ground
With walls and towers were girdled round;
And there were gardens bright with sinuous rills,
Where blossomed many an incense-bearing tree;
And here were forests ancient as the hills,   10
Enfolding sunny spots of greenery.

But oh! that deep romantic chasm which slanted
Down the green hill athwart a cedarn cover!
A savage place! as holy and enchanted
As e'er beneath a waning moon was haunted   15
By woman wailing for her demon-lover!
And from this chasm, with ceaseless turmoil seething,
As if this earth in fast thick pants were breathing,
A mighty fountain momently was forced:
Amid whose swift half-intermitted burst   20

Kubla Khan ruler of China (1216–1294)

Huge fragments vaulted like rebounding hail,
Or chaffy grain beneath the thresher's flail:
And 'mid these dancing rocks at once and ever
It flung up momently the sacred river.
Five miles meandering with a mazy motion   25
Through wood and dale the sacred river ran,
Then reached the caverns measureless to man,
And sank in tumult to a lifeless ocean:
And 'mid this tumult Kubla heard from far
Ancestral voices prophesying war!   30

    The shadow of the dome of pleasure
    Floated midway on the waves;
    Where was heard the mingled measure
    From the fountain and the caves.
It was a miracle of rare device,   35
A sunny pleasure-dome with caves of ice!

    A damsel with a dulcimer
    In a vision once I saw:
    It was an Abyssinian maid,
    And on her dulcimer she played,   40
    Singing of Mount Abora.
    Could I revive within me
    Her symphony and song,
    To such a deep delight 'twould win me,
That with music loud and long,   45
I would build that dome in air,
That sunny dome! those caves of ice!
And all who heard should see them there,
And all should cry, Beware! Beware!
His flashing eyes, his floating hair!   50
Weave a circle round him thrice,
And close your eyes with holy dread,
For he on honey-dew hath fed,
And drunk the milk of Paradise.

    (1797–1798)

George Gordon, Lord Byron
1788–1824

WHEN WE TWO PARTED 🎵

When we two parted
  In silence and tears,
Half broken-hearted
  To sever for years,
Pale grew thy cheek and cold,   5
  Colder thy kiss;
Truly that hour foretold
  Sorrow to this.

The dew of the morning
  Sunk chill on my brow—   10
It felt like the warning
  Of what I feel now.
Thy vows are all broken,
  And light is thy fame;
I hear thy name spoken,   15
  And share in its shame.

They name thee before me,
  A knell to mine ear;
A shudder comes o'er me—
  Why wert thou so dear?   20
They know not I knew thee,
  Who knew thee too well:—
Long, long shall I rue thee,
  Too deeply to tell.

In secret we met—   25
  In silence I grieve
That thy heart could forget,
  Thy spirit deceive.
If I should meet thee
  After long years,   30
How should I greet thee?—
  With silence and tears.

    —1813

SHE WALKS IN BEAUTY 🔲

From Hebrew Melodies

I

She walks in Beauty, like the night
   Of cloudless climes and starry skies;
And all that's best of dark and bright
   Meet in her aspect and her eyes:
Thus mellowed to that tender light   5
   Which Heaven to gaudy day denies.

II

One shade the more, one ray the less,
   Had half impaired the nameless grace
Which waves in every raven trees,
   Or softly lightens o'er her face;   10
Where thoughts serenely sweet express,
   How pure, how dear their dwelling-place.

III

And on that cheek, and o'er that brow,
   So soft, so calm, yet eloquent,
The smiles that win, the tints that glow,   15
   But tell of days in goodness spent,
A mind at peace with all below,
   A heart whose love is innocent!

    —1814

Percy Bysshe Shelley
1792 – 1822

OZYMANDIAS 🔊

I met a traveler from an antique land
Who said: Two vast and trunkless legs of stone
Stand in the desert. . . . Near them, on the sand,
Half sunk, a shattered visage lies, whose frown,
And wrinkled lip, and sneer of cold command,   5
Tell that its sculptor well those passions read
Which yet survive, stamped on these lifeless things,
The hand that mocked them, and the heart that fed:
And on the pedestal these words appear:
"My name is Ozymandias, king of kings: 10
Look on my works, ye Mighty, and despair!"
Nothing beside remains. Round the decay
Of that colossal wreck, boundless and bare
The lone and level sands stretch far away.

　　　—1818

ODE TO THE WEST WIND 🔊

I

O wild West Wind, thou breath of Autumn's being,
Thou, from whose unseen presence the leaves dead
Are driven, like ghosts from an enchanter fleeing,

Yellow, and black, and pale, and hectic red,
Pestilence-stricken multitudes: O thou,   5
Who chariotest to their dark wintry bed

The wingèd seeds, where they lie cold and low,
Each like a corpse within its grave, until
Thine azure sister of the Spring shall blow

Her clarion o'er the dreaming earth, and fill   10
(Driving sweet buds like flocks to feed in air)
With living hues and odors plain and hill:

Wild Spirit, which art moving everywhere;
Destroyer and preserver; hear, oh, hear!

2

Thou on whose stream, mid the steep sky's commotion,   15
Loose clouds like earth's decaying leaves are shed,
Shook from the tangled boughs of Heaven and Ocean,

Angels of rain and lightning: there are spread
On the blue surface of thine aëry surge,
Like the bright hair uplifted from the head   20

Of some fierce Mænad,° even from the dim verge
Of the horizon to the zenith's height,
The locks of the approaching storm. Thou dirge

Of the dying year, to which this closing night
Will be the dome of a vast sepulcher,   25
Vaulted with all thy congregated might

Of vapors, from whose solid atmosphere
Black rain, and fire, and hail will burst: oh, hear!

3

Thou who didst waken from his summer dreams
The blue Mediterranean, where he lay,   30
Lulled by the coil of his crystàlline streams,

Beside a pumice isle in Baiae's bay,°
And saw in sleep old palaces and towers
Quivering within the wave's intenser day,

All overgrown with azure moss and flowers   35
So sweet, the sense faints picturing them! Thou
For whose path the Atlantic's level powers

Cleave themselves into chasms, while far below
The sea-blooms and the oozy woods which wear
The sapless foliage of the ocean, know   40

Thy voice, and suddenly grow gray with fear,
And tremble and despoil themselves: oh, hear!

---

21 **Mænad** female worshipper of Bacchus, god of wine   32 **Baiae's bay** near Naples

4

If I were a dead leaf thou mightest bear;
If I were a swift cloud to fly with thee;
A wave to pant beneath thy power, and share   45

The impulse of thy strength, only less free
Than thou, O uncontrollable! If even
I were as in my boyhood, and could be

The comrade of thy wanderings over Heaven,
As then, when to outstrip thy skyey speed   50
Scarce seemed a vision; I would ne'er have striven

As thus with thee in prayer in my sore need.
Oh, lift me as a wave, a leaf, a cloud!
I fall upon the thorns of life! I bleed!

A heavy weight of hours has chained and bowed   55
One too like thee: tameless, and swift, and proud.

5

Make me thy lyre, even as the forest is:
What if my leaves are falling like its own!
The tumult of thy mighty harmonies

Will take from both a deep, autumnal tone,   60
Sweet though in sadness. Be thou, Spirit fierce,
My spirit! Be thou me, impetuous one!

Drive my dead thoughts over the universe
Like withered leaves to quicken a new birth!
And, by the incantation of this verse,   65

Scatter, as from an unextinguished hearth
Ashes and sparks, my words among mankind!
Be through my lips to unawakened earth

The trumpet of a prophecy! O Wind,
If Winter comes, can Spring be far behind?   70

—1820

John Keats
1795 – 1821

WHEN I HAVE FEARS THAT I MAY CEASE TO BE 🔊

When I have fears that I may cease to be
    Before my pen has gleaned my teeming brain,
Before high-pilèd books, in charact'ry,°
    Hold like rich garners the full-ripened grain;
When I behold, upon the night's starred face,   5
    Huge cloudy symbols of a high romance,
And think that I may never live to trace
    Their shadows with the magic hand of chance;
And when I feel, fair creature of an hour,
    That I shall never look upon thee more,   10
Never have relish in the fairy power
    Of unreflecting love—then on the shore
Of the wide world I stand alone, and think
    Till love and fame to nothingness do sink.

(1818)

TO AUTUMN 🔊

I

Season of mists and mellow fruitfulness,
    Close bosom-friend of the maturing sun;
Conspiring with him how to load and bless
    With fruit the vines that round the thatch-eaves run;
To bend with apples the mossed cottage-trees,   5
    And fill all fruit with ripeness to the core;
        To swell the gourd, and plump the hazel shells
    With a sweet kernel; to set budding more,
    And still more, later flowers for the bees,
    Until they think warm days will never cease,   10
        For Summer has o'er-brimmed their clammy cells.

---

3 charact'ry writing

II

Who hath not seen thee oft amid thy store?
   Sometimes whoever seeks abroad may find
Thee sitting careless on a granary floor,
   Thy hair soft-lifted by the winnowing wind;   15
Or on a half-reaped furrow sound asleep,
   Drowsed with the fume of poppies, while thy hook°
     Spares the next swath and all its twinèd flowers:
And sometimes like a gleaner thou dost keep
   Steady thy laden head across a brook;   20
   Or by a cider-press, with patient look,
     Thou watchest the last oozings hours by hours.

III

Where are the songs of Spring? Ay, where are they?
   Think not of them, thou hast thy music too,—
While barrèd clouds bloom the soft-dying day,   25
   And touch the stubble-plains with rosy hue;
Then in a wailful choir the small gnats mourn
   Among the river sallows,° borne aloft
     Or sinking as the light wind lives or dies;
And full-grown lambs loud bleat from hilly bourn;   30
Hedge-crickets sing; and now with treble soft
The red-breast whistles from a garden-croft°
   And gathering swallows twitter in the skies.

   —1820

ODE ON A GRECIAN URN 🔊

Thou still unravished bride of quietness,
   Thou foster-child of silence and slow time,
Sylvan historian, who canst thus express
   A flowery tale more sweetly than our rhyme:
What leaf-fringed legend haunts about thy shape   5
   Of deities or mortals, or of both,
     In Tempe or the dales of Arcady?
   What men or gods are these? What maidens loth?
What mad pursuit? What struggle to escape?
     What pipes and timbrels? What wild ecstasy?   10

---

17 hook sickle   **28 sallows** willows   **32 garden-croft** enclosed garden

Heard melodies are sweet, but those unheard
    Are sweeter; therefore, ye soft pipes, play on;
Not to the sensual ear, but, more endeared,
    Pipe to the spirit ditties of no tone:
Fair youth, beneath the trees, thou canst not leave   15
    Thy song, nor ever can those trees be bare;
        Bold Lover, never, never canst thou kiss,
Though winning near the goal—yet, do not grieve;
        She cannot fade, though thou hast not thy bliss,
For ever wilt thou love, and she be fair!   20

Ah, happy, happy boughs! that cannot shed
    Your leaves, nor ever bid the Spring adieu;
And, happy melodist, unwearièd,
    For ever piping songs for ever new;
More happy love! more happy, happy love!   25
    For ever warm and still to be enjoyed,
        For ever panting, and for ever young;
All breathing human passion far above,
    That leaves a heart high-sorrowful and cloyed,
        A burning forehead, and a parching tongue.   30

Who are these coming to the sacrifice?
    To what green altar, O mysterious priest,
Lead'st thou that heifer lowing at the skies,
    And all her silken flanks with garlands drest?
What little town by river or sea shore,   35
    Or mountain-built with peaceful citadel,
        Is emptied of this folk, this pious morn?
And, little town, thy streets for evermore
    Will silent be; and not a soul to tell
        Why thou art desolate, can e'er return.   40

O Attic shape! Fair attitude! with brede°
    Of marble men and maidens overwrought,
With forest branches and the trodden weed;
    Thou, silent form, dost tease us out of thought
As doth Eternity: Cold Pastoral!   45
    When old age shall this generation waste,
        Thou shalt remain, in midst of other woe
Than ours, a friend to man, to whom thou say'st,
Beauty is truth, truth beauty,—that is all
    Ye know on earth, and all ye need to know.   50

    —1820

---

41 brede woven or braided design

Elizabeth Barrett Browning
1806–1861

HOW DO I LOVE THEE? LET ME COUNT THE WAYS 🔊

How do I love thee? Let me count the ways.
I love thee to the depth and breadth and height
My soul can reach, when feeling out of sight
For the ends of being and ideal grace.
I love thee to the level of every day's   5
Most quiet need, by sun and candle-light.
I love thee freely, as men strive for right.
I love thee purely, as they turn from praise.
I love thee with the passion put to use
In my old griefs, and with my childhood's faith.   10
I love thee with a love I seemed to lose
With my lost saints. I love thee with the breath,
Smiles, tears, of all my life; and, if God choose,
I shall but love thee better after death.

    —1850

Edgar Allan Poe
1809–1849

TO HELEN 🔊

Helen, thy beauty is to me
  Like those Nicean barks of yore,
That gently, o'er a perfumed sea,
  The weary, way-worn wanderer bore
  To his own native shore.   5

On desperate seas long wont to roam,
   Thy hyacinth hair, thy classic face,
Thy Naiad airs have brought me home
   To the glory that was Greece
And the grandeur that was Rome.   10

Lo! in yon brilliant window-niche
   How statue-like I see thee stand!
   The agate lamp within thy hand,
Ah! Psyche, from the regions which
   Are Holy Land!   15

    —1831

THE RAVEN

Once upon a midnight dreary, while I pondered, weak and weary,
Over many a quaint and curious volume of forgotten lore—
While I nodded, nearly napping, suddenly there came a tapping,
As of some one gently rapping, rapping at my chamber door.
" 'Tis some visitor," I muttered, "tapping at my chamber door—   5
                  Only this and nothing more."

Ah, distinctly I remember it was in the bleak December;
And each separate dying ember wrought its ghost upon the floor.
Eagerly I wished the morrow;—vainly I had sought to borrow
From my books surcease of sorrow—sorrow for the lost Lenore— 10
For the rare and radiant maiden whom the angels name Lenore—
                  Nameless *here* for evermore.

And the silken, sad, uncertain rustling of each purple curtain
Thrilled me—filled me with fantastic terrors never felt before;
So that now, to still the beating of my heart, I stood repeating 15
" 'Tis some visitor entreating entrance at my chamber door;—
Some late visitor entreating entrance at my chamber door;—
                  This it is and nothing more."

Presently my soul grew stronger; hesitating then no longer,
"Sir," said I, "or Madam, truly your forgiveness I implore; 20
But the fact is I was napping, and so gently you came rapping,
And so faintly you came tapping, tapping at my chamber door,
That I scarce was sure I heard you"—here I opened wide the door;—
                  Darkness there and nothing more.

Deep into that darkness peering, long I stood there wondering,
    fearing,   25
Doubting, dreaming dreams no mortal ever dared to dream before;
But the silence was unbroken, and the stillness gave no token,
And the only word there spoken was the whispered word, "Lenore?"
This I whispered, and an echo murmured back the word, "Lenore!"
                  Merely this and nothing more.   30

Back into the chamber turning, all my soul within me burning,
Soon again I heard a tapping somewhat louder than before.
"Surely," said I, "surely that is something at my window lattice;
Let me see, then, what thereat is, and this mystery explore—
Let my heart be still a moment and this mystery explore;—   35
                'Tis the wind and nothing more!"

Open here I flung the shutter, when, with many a flirt and flutter,
In there stepped a stately Raven of the saintly days of yore;
Not the least obeisance made he; not a minute stopped or stayed he;
But, with mien of lord or lady, perched above my chamber door—   40
Perched upon a bust of Pallas° just above my chamber door—
                Perched, and sat, and nothing more.

Then this ebony bird beguiling my sad fancy into smiling,
By the grave and stern decorum of the countenance it wore,
"Though thy crest be shorn and shaven, thou," I said, "art sure
    no craven,   45
Ghastly grim and ancient Raven wandering from the Nightly shore—
Tell me what thy lordly name is on the Night's Plutonian° shore!"
              Quoth the Raven, "Nevermore."

Much I marvelled this ungainly fowl to hear discourse so plainly,
Though its answer little meaning—little relevancy bore;   50
For we cannot help agreeing that no living human being
Ever yet was blessed with seeing bird above his chamber door—
Bird or beast upon the sculptured bust above his chamber door,
           With such name as "Nevermore."

But the Raven, sitting lonely on the placid bust, spoke only   55
That one word, as if his soul in that one word he did outpour.
Nothing farther then he uttered—not a feather then he fluttered—
Till I scarcely more than muttered, "Other friends have flown before—
On the morrow *he* will leave me, as my Hopes have flown before."
           Then the bird said, "Nevermore."   60

---

41 Pallas Athena, goddess of wisdom   **47 Plutonian** after Pluto, Roman god of the
underworld

Startled at the stillness broken by reply so aptly spoken,
"Doubtless," said I, "what it utters is its only stock and store
Caught from some unhappy master whom unmerciful Disaster
Followed fast and followed faster till his songs one burden bore—
Till the dirges of his Hope that melancholy burden bore   65
                   Of 'Never—nevermore.' "

But the Raven still beguiling all my sad fancy into smiling,
Straight I wheeled a cushioned seat in front of bird and bust and door;
Then, upon the velvet sinking, I betook myself to linking
Fancy unto fancy, thinking what this ominous bird of yore—   70
What this grim, ungainly, ghastly, gaunt, and ominous bird of yore
                  Meant in croaking "Nevermore."

This I sat engaged in guessing, but no syllable expressing
To the fowl whose fiery eyes now burned into my bosom's core;
This and more I sat divining, with my head at ease reclining   75
On the cushion's velvet lining that the lamp-light gloated o'er,
But whose velvet-violet lining with the lamp-light gloating o'er,
                 She shall press, ah, nevermore!

Then, methought, the air grew denser, perfumed from an unseen
    censer
Swung by seraphim whose foot-falls tinkled on the tufted floor.   80
"Wretch," I cried, "thy God hath lent thee—by these angels he
    hath sent thee.
Respite—respite and nepenthe° from thy memories of Lenore;
Quaff, oh quaff this kind nepenthe and forget this lost Lenore!"
               Quoth the Raven, "Nevermore."

"Prophet!" said I, "thing of evil!—prophet still, if bird or devil!—   85
Whether Tempter sent, or whether tempest tossed thee here
    ashore,
Desolate yet all undaunted, on this desert land enchanted—
On this home by Horror haunted—tell me truly, I implore—
Is there—*is* there balm in Gilead?—tell me—tell me, I implore!"
              Quoth the Raven, "Nevermore." 90

"Prophet!" said I, "thing of evil!—prophet still, if bird or devil!
By that Heaven that bends above us—by that God we both adore—
Tell this soul with sorrow laden if, within the distant Aidenn,°
It shall clasp a sainted maiden whom the angels name Lenore—
Clasp a rare and radiant maiden whom the angels name Lenore."   95
              Quoth the Raven, "Nevermore."

---

82 **nepenthe** drug causing forgetfulness   93 **Aidenn** Eden

"Be that word our sign of parting, bird or fiend!" I shrieked,
    upstarting—
"Get thee back into the tempest and the Night's Plutonian shore!
Leave no black plume as a token of that lie thy soul hath spoken!
Leave my loneliness unbroken!—quit the bust above my door!   100
Take thy beak from out my heart, and take thy form from off
    my door!"
                    Quoth the Raven, "Nevermore."

And the Raven, never flitting, still is sitting, *still* is sitting
On the pallid bust of Pallas just above my chamber door;
And his eyes have all the seeming of a demon's that is dreaming,   105
And the lamp-light o'er him streaming throws his shadow on the
    floor;
And my soul from out that shadow that lies floating on the floor
                    Shall be lifted—nevermore!

—1845

Alfred, Lord Tennyson
1809–1892

ULYSSES

It little profits that an idle king,
By this still hearth, among these barren crags,
Matched with an agèd wife, I mete and dole
Unequal laws unto a savage race,
That hoard, and sleep, and feed, and know not me.   5
I cannot rest from travel; I will drink
Life to the lees. All times I have enjoyed
Greatly, have suffered greatly, both with those
That loved me, and alone; on shore, and when
Through scudding drifts the rainy Hyades   10
Vexed the dim sea. I am become a name;
For always roaming with a hungry heart
Much have I seen and known—cities of men
And manners, climates, councils, governments,

Myself not least, but honored of them all—   15
And drunk delight of battle with my peers,
Far on the ringing plains of windy Troy.
I am a part of all that I have met;
Yet all experience is an arch wherethrough
Gleams that untraveled world whose margin fades   20
Forever and forever when I move.
How dull it is to pause, to make an end,
To rust unburnished, not to shine in use!
As though to breathe were life! Life piled on life
Were all too little, and of one to me   25
Little remains; but every hour is saved
From that eternal silence, something more,
A bringer of new things; and vile it were
For some three suns to store and hoard myself,
And this grey spirit yearning in desire   30
To follow knowledge like a sinking star,
Beyond the utmost bound of human thought.
        This is my son, mine own Telemachus,
To whom I leave the scepter and the isle—
Well-loved of me, discerning to fulfill   35
This labor, by slow prudence to make mild
A rugged people, and through soft degrees
Subdue them to the useful and the good.
Most blameless is he, centered in the sphere
Of common duties, decent not to fail   40
In offices of tenderness, and pay
Meet adoration to my household gods,
When I am gone. He works his work, I mine.
        There lies the port; the vessel puffs her sail;
There gloom the dark, broad seas. My mariners,   45
Souls that have toiled, and wrought, and thought with me—
That ever with a frolic welcome took
The thunder and the sunshine, and opposed
Free hearts, free foreheads—you and I are old;
Old age hath yet his honor and his toil.   50
Death closes all; but something ere the end,
Some work of noble note, may yet be done,
Not unbecoming men that strove with Gods.
The lights begin to twinkle from the rocks;
The long day wanes; the low moon climbs; the deep   55
Moans round with many voices. Come, my friends,
'Tis not too late to seek a newer world.
Push off, and sitting well in order smite
The sounding furrows; for my purpose holds
To sail beyond the sunset, and the baths   60

Of all the western stars, until I die.
It may be that the gulfs will wash us down;
It may be we shall touch the Happy Isles,°
And see the great Achilles, whom we knew.
Though much is taken, much abides; and though   65
We are not now that strength which in old days
Moved earth and heaven, that which we are, we are—
One equal temper of heroic hearts,
Made weak by time and fate, but strong in will
To strive, to seek, to find, and not to yield.   70

(1833)

TEARS, IDLE TEARS 🔊

Tears, idle tears, I know not what they mean,
Tears from the depth of some divine despair
Rise in the heart, and gather to the eyes,
In looking on the happy autumn-fields,
And thinking of the days that are no more.   5

Fresh as the first beam glittering on a sail,
That brings our friends up from the underworld,
Sad as the last which reddens over one
That sinks with all we love below the verge;
So sad, so fresh, the days that are no more.   10

Ah, sad and strange as in dark summer dawns
The earliest pipe of half-awakened birds
To dying ears, when unto dying eyes
The casement slowly grows a glimmering square;
So sad, so strange, the days that are no more.   15

Dear as remembered kisses after death,
And sweet as those by hopeless fancy feigned
On lips that are for others; deep as love,
Deep as first love, and wild with all regret;
O Death in Life, the days that are no more!   20

—1847

---

63 **Happy Isles** Elysium, a paradise

Robert Browning
1812–1889

MY LAST DUCHESS 🎵

Ferrara

That's my last Duchess painted on the wall,
Looking as if she were alive. I call
That piece a wonder, now: Frà Pandolf's hands
Worked busily a day, and there she stands.
Will 't please you sit and look at her? I said   5
"Frà Pandolf" by design, for never read
Strangers like you that pictured countenance,
The depth and passion of its earnest glance,
But to myself they turned (since none puts by
The curtain I have drawn for you, but I)   10
And seemed as they would ask me, if they durst,
How such a glance came there; so, not the first
Are you to turn and ask thus. Sir, 'twas not
Her husband's presence only, called that spot
Of joy into the Duchess' cheek; perhaps   15
Frà Pandolf chanced to say "Her mantle laps
Over my lady's wrist too much," or "Paint
Must never hope to reproduce the faint
Half-flush that dies along her throat." Such stuff
Was courtesy, she thought, and cause enough   20
For calling up that spot of joy. She had
A heart—how shall I say?—too soon made glad,
Too easily impressed; she liked whate'er
She looked on, and her looks went everywhere.
Sir, 'twas all one! My favor at her breast,   25
The dropping of the daylight in the West,
The bough of cherries some officious fool
Broke in the orchard for her, the white mule
She rode with round the terrace—all and each
Would draw from her alike the approving speech,   30
Or blush, at least. She thanked men,—good! but thanked
Somehow—I know not how—as if she ranked
My gift of a nine-hundred-years-old name
With anybody's gift. Who'd stoop to blame
This sort of trifling? Even had you skill   35
In speech—which I have not—to make your will

Quite clear to such an one, and say "Just this
Or that in you disgusts me; here you miss,
Or there exceed the mark"—and if she let
Herself be lessoned so, nor plainly set   40
Her wits to yours, forsooth, and made excuse—
E'en then would be some stooping; and I choose
Never to stoop. Oh sir, she smiled, no doubt,
Whene'er I passed her; but who passed without
Much the same smile? This grew; I gave commands;   45
Then all smiles stopped together. There she stands
As if alive. Will 't please you rise? We'll meet
The company below, then. I repeat,
The Count your master's known munificence
Is ample warrant that no just pretense   50
Of mine for dowry will be disallowed;
Though his fair daughter's self, as I avowed
At starting, is my object. Nay, we'll go
Together down, sir. Notice Neptune, though,
Taming a sea-horse, thought a rarity,   55
Which Claus of Innsbruck cast in bronze for me!

—1842

Walt Whitman
1819–1892

SONG OF MYSELF, 6 🔊

A child said *What is the grass?* fetching it to me with full hands;
How could I answer the child? I do not know what it is any more
    than he.

I guess it must be the flag of my disposition, out of hopeful green
    stuff woven.

Or I guess it is the handkerchief of the Lord,
A scented gift and remembrancer designedly dropped,   5
Bearing the owner's name someway in the corners, that we may
    see and remark, and say *Whose?*

Or I guess the grass is itself a child, the produced babe of the
   vegetation.

Or I guess it is a uniform hieroglyphic,
And it means, Sprouting alike in broad zones and narrow zones,
Growing among black folks as among white,   10
Kanuck,° Tuckahoe,° Congressman, Cuff,° I give them the same,
   I receive them the same.

And now it seems to me the beautiful uncut hair of graves.

Tenderly will I use you curling grass,
It may be you transpire from the breasts of young men,
It may be if I had known them I would have loved them,   15
It may be you are from old people, or from offspring taken soon
   out of their mothers' laps,
And here you are the mothers' laps.

This grass is very dark to be from the white heads of old mothers.
Darker than the colorless beards of old men.
Dark to come from under the faint red roofs of mouths.   20

O I perceive after all so many uttering tongues,
And I perceive they do not come from the roofs of mouths for
   nothing.

I wish I could translate the hints about the dead young men and
   women,
And the hints about old men and mothers, and the offspring
   taken soon out of their laps.

What do you think has become of the young and old men?   25
And what do you think has become of the women and children?

They are alive and well somewhere,
The smallest sprout shows there is really no death,
And if ever there was it led forward life, and does not wait at the end
   to arrest it.
And ceased the moment life appeared.   30

All goes onward and outward, nothing collapses.
And to die is different from what anyone supposed, and luckier.

   —1855

---

11 **Kanuck** French-Canadian   **Tuckahoe** coastal Virginian   **Cuff** a black slave

WHEN I HEARD THE LEARN'D ASTRONOMER 🔊

When I heard the learn'd astronomer,
When the proofs, the figures, were ranged in columns before me,
When I was shown the charts and diagrams, to add, divide, and
    measure them,
When I sitting heard the astronomer where he lectured with much
    applause in the lecture-room,
How soon unaccountable I became tired and sick,   5
Till rising and gliding out I wander'd off by myself,
In the mystical moist night-air, and from time to time,
Look'd up in perfect silence at the stars.

    —1865

CAVALRY CROSSING A FORD 🔊

A line in long array where they wind betwixt green islands,
They take a serpentine course, their arms flash in the sun—hark to
    the musical clank,
Behold the silvery river, in it the splashing horses loitering stop to
    drink,
Behold the brown-faced men, each group, each person a picture, the
    negligent rest on the saddles,
Some emerge on the opposite bank, others are just entering the
    ford—while,   5
Scarlet and blue and snowy white,
The guidon flags flutter gayly in the wind.

    (1865)

A NOISELESS PATIENT SPIDER 🔃

A noiseless patient spider,
I mark'd where on a little promontory it stood isolated,
Mark'd how to explore the vacant vast surrounding,
It launch'd forth filament, filament, filament, out of itself,
Ever unreeling them, ever tirelessly speeding them.   5
And you O my soul where you stand,
Surrounded, detached, in measureless oceans of space,
Ceaselessly musing, venturing, throwing, seeking the spheres to
    connect them,
Till the bridge you will need be form'd, till the ductile anchor hold,
Till the gossamer thread you fling catch somewhere, O my soul.   10

(1876)

Matthew Arnold
1822–1888

DOVER BEACH 🔃

The sea is calm tonight.
The tide is full, the moon lies fair
Upon the straits; on the French coast the light
Gleams and is gone; the cliffs of England stand,
Glimmering and vast, out in the tranquil bay.   5
Come to the window, sweet is the night-air!
Only, from the long line of spray
Where the sea meets the moon-blanched land,
Listen! you hear the grating roar
Of pebbles which the waves draw back, and fling,   10
At their return, up the high strand,
Begin, and cease, and then again begin,
With tremulous cadence slow, and bring
The eternal note of sadness in.

Sophocles long ago   15
Heard it on the Aegean, and it brought

Into his mind the turbid ebb and flow
Of human misery; we
Find also in the sound a thought,
Hearing it by this distant northern sea.   20

The Sea of Faith
Was once, too, at the full, and round earth's shore
Lay like the folds of a bright girdle furled.
But now I only hear
Its melancholy, long, withdrawing roar,   25
Retreating, to the breath
Of the night-wind, down the vast edges drear
And naked shingles of the world.

Ah, love, let us be true
To one another! for the world, which seems   30
To lie before us like a land of dreams,
So various, so beautiful, so new,
Hath really neither joy, nor love, nor light,
Nor certitude, nor peace, nor help for pain;
And we are here as on a darkling plain   35
Swept with confused alarms of struggle and flight,
Where ignorant armies clash by night.

   —1867

Christina Rossetti
1 8 3 0 – 1 8 9 4

UPHILL

Does the road wind uphill all the way?
   Yes, to the very end.
Will the day's journey take the whole long day?
   From morn to night, my friend.

But is there for the night a resting-place?   5
   A roof for when the slow dark hours begin.

May not the darkness hide it from my face?
    You cannot miss that inn.

Shall I meet other wayfarers at night?
    Those who have gone before.   10
Then must I knock, or call when just in sight?
    They will not keep you standing at that door.

Shall I find comfort, travel-sore and weak?
    Of labor you shall find the sum.
Will there be beds for me and all who seek?   15
    Yea, beds for all who come.

    —1862

Emily Dickinson
1 8 3 0 – 1 8 8 6

WILD NIGHTS—WILD NIGHTS!

Wild Nights—Wild Nights!
Were I with thee
Wild Nights should be
Our luxury!

Futile—the Winds—   5
To a Heart in port—
Done with the Compass—
Done with the Chart!

Rowing in Eden—
Ah, the Sea!   10
Might I but moor—Tonight—
In Thee!

    (ca. 1861)

THE SOUL SELECTS HER OWN SOCIETY

The Soul selects her own Society—
Then—shuts the Door—
To her divine Majority—
Present no more—

Unmoved—she notes the Chariots—pausing—   5
At her low Gate—
Unmoved—an Emperor be kneeling
Upon her Mat—

I've known her—from an ample nation—
Choose One—   10
Then—close the Valves of her attention—
Like Stone—

    (ca. 1862)

I HEARD A FLY BUZZ— WHEN I DIED

I heard a Fly buzz—when I died—
The Stillness in the Room
Was like the Stillness in the Air—
Between the Heaves of Storm—

The Eyes around—had wrung them dry—   5
And Breaths were gathering firm
For that last Onset—when the King
Be witnessed—in the Room—

I willed my Keepsakes—Signed away
What portion of me be   10
Assignable—and then it was
There interposed a Fly—

With Blue—uncertain stumbling Buzz—
Between the light—and me—
And then the Windows failed—and then   15
I could not see to see—

    (ca. 1862)

AFTER GREAT PAIN,
A FORMAL FEELING COMES

After great pain, a formal feeling comes—
The Nerves sit ceremonious, like Tombs—
The stiff Heart questions was it He, that bore,
And Yesterday, or Centuries before?

The Feet, mechanical, go round—   5
Of Ground, or Air, or Ought—
A Wooden way
Regardless grown,
A Quartz contentment, like a stone—

This is the Hour of Lead—   10
Remembered, if outlived,
As Freezing persons, recollect the Snow—
First—Chill—then Stupor—then the letting go—

    (1862)

Thomas Hardy
1840–1928

NEUTRAL TONES

We stood by a pond that winter day,
And the sun was white, as though chidden of God,
And a few leaves lay on the starving sod;
    —They had fallen from an ash, and were gray.

Your eyes on me were as eyes that rove   5
Over tedious riddles of years ago;
And some words played between us to and fro
    On which lost the more by our love.

The smile on your mouth was the deadest thing
Alive enough to have strength to die;   10
And a grin of bitterness swept thereby
      Like an ominous bird a-wing . . .

Since then, keen lessons that love deceives,
And wrings with wrong, have shaped to me
Your face, and the God-curst sun, and a tree,   15
      And a pond edged with grayish leaves.

    —1898

THE MAN HE KILLED

"Had he and I but met
    By some old ancient inn,
We should have sat us down to wet
    Right many a nipperkin!°

"But ranged as infantry,   5
    And staring face to face,
I shot at him as he at me,
    And killed him in his place.

"I shot him dead because—
    Because he was my foe,   10
Just so: my foe of course he was;
    That's clear enough; although

"He thought he'd 'list, perhaps,
    Off-hand like—just as I—
Was out of work—had sold his traps°—   15
    No other reason why.

"Yes; quaint and curious war is!
    You shoot a fellow down
You'd treat if met where any bar is,
    Or help to half-a-crown."   20

    —1909

---

4 nipperkin a measure of beer or wine   **15 traps** possessions

Gerard Manley Hopkins
1844–1889

GOD'S GRANDEUR 🔊

The world is charged with the grandeur of God.
   It will flame out, like shining from shook foil;
   It gathers to a greatness, like the ooze of oil
Crushed. Why do men then now not reck his rod?
Generations have trod, have trod, have trod;   5
   And all is seared with trade; bleared, smeared with toil;
   And wears man's smudge and shares man's smell: the soil
Is bare now, nor can foot feel, being shod.

And for all this, nature is never spent;
   There lives the dearest freshness deep down things;   10
And though the last lights off the black West went
   Oh, morning, at the brown brink eastward, springs—
Because the Holy Ghost over the bent
   World broods with warm breast and with ah! bright wings.

   (1877)

PIED° BEAUTY 🔊

Glory be to God for dappled things—
   For skies of couple-colour as a brinded° cow;
      For rose-moles all in stipple upon trout that swim;
Fresh-firecoal chestnut-falls; finches' wings;
   Landscape plotted and pieced—fold, fallow, and plough;   5
      And áll trádes, their gear and tackle and trim.
All things counter, original, spare, strange;
   Whatever is fickle, freckled (who knows how?)
      With swift, slow; sweet, sour; adazzle, dim;
He fathers-forth whose beauty is past change: 10
                   Praise him.

   (1877)

---

pied variegated   **2 brinded** streaked

A. E. Housman
1859–1936

TO AN ATHLETE DYING YOUNG 🝿

The time you won your town the race
We chaired you through the market-place;
Man and boy stood cheering by,
And home we brought you shoulder-high.

To-day, the road all runners come,   5
Shoulder high we bring you home,
And set you at your threshold down,
Townsman of a stiller town.

Smart lad, to slip betimes away
From fields where glory does not stay   10
And early though the laurel grows
It withers quicker than the rose.

Eyes the shady night has shut
Cannot see the record cut,
And silence sounds no worse than cheers   15
After earth has stopped the ears:

Now you will not swell the rout
Of lads that wore their honours out,
Runners whom renown outran
And the name died before the man.   20

So set, before its echoes fade,
The fleet foot on the sill of shade,
And hold to the low lintel up
The still-defended challenge-cup.

And round that early-laurelled head   25
Will flock to gaze the strengthless dead,
And find unwithered on its curls
The garland briefer than a girl's.

  —1896

LOVELIEST OF TREES,
THE CHERRY NOW ◍

Loveliest of trees, the cherry now
Is hung with bloom along the bough,
And stands about the woodland ride
Wearing white for Eastertide.

Now, of my threescore years and ten,   5
Twenty will not come again,
And take from seventy springs a score,
It only leaves me fifty more.

And since to look at things in bloom
Fifty springs are little room,   10
About the woodlands I will go
To see the cherry hung with snow.

    —1896

William Butler Yeats
1865–1939

THE LAKE ISLE OF INNISFREE ◍

I will arise and go now, and go to Innisfree,
And a small cabin build there, of clay and wattles made:
Nine bean-rows will I have there, a hive for the honey-bee,
And live alone in the bee-loud glade.

And I shall have some peace there, for peace comes dropping slow,   5
Dropping from the veils of the morning to where the cricket sings;
There midnight's all a glimmer, and noon a purple glow,
And evening full of the linnet's wings.

I will arise and go now, for always night and day
I hear lake water lapping with low sounds by the shore;   10

While I stand on the roadway, or on the pavements gray,
I hear it in the deep heart's core.
    —1892

WHEN YOU ARE OLD 🎵

When you are old and grey and full of sleep,
And nodding by the fire, take down this book,
And slowly read, and dream of the soft look
Your eyes had once, and of their shadows deep;

How many loved your moments of glad grace,   5
And loved your beauty with love false or true,
But one man loved the pilgrim soul in you,
And loved the sorrows of your changing face;

And bending down beside the glowing bars,
Murmur, a little sadly, how Love fled   10
And paced upon the mountains overhead
And hid his face amid a crowd of stars.
    —1893

THE SECOND COMING° 🎵

Turning and turning in the widening gyre°
The falcon cannot hear the falconer;
Things fall apart; the center cannot hold;
Mere anarchy is loosed upon the world,
The blood-dimmed tide is loosed, and everywhere   5
The ceremony of innocence is drowned;
The best lack all conviction, while the worst
Are full of passionate intensity.

Surely some revelation is at hand;
Surely the Second Coming is at hand;   10
The Second Coming! Hardly are those words out
When a vast image out of *Spiritus Mundi*
Troubles my sight: somewhere in the sands of the desert

The Second Coming the return of Christ as prophesied in the Book of Revelation
1 gyre spiral

A shape with lion body and the head of a man,
A gaze blank and pitiless as the sun,   15
Is moving its slow thighs, while all about it
Reel shadows of the indignant desert birds.
The darkness drops again; but now I know
That twenty centuries of stony sleep
Were vexed to nightmare by a rocking cradle,   20
And what rough beast, its hour come round at last,
Slouches towards Bethlehem to be born?

    —1921

SAILING TO BYZANTIUM

That is no country for old men. The young
In one another's arms, birds in the trees
—Those dying generations—at their song,
The salmon-falls, the mackerel-crowded seas,
Fish, flesh, or fowl, commend all summer long   5
Whatever is begotten, born, and dies.
Caught in that sensual music all neglect
Monuments of unaging intellect.

An aged man is but a paltry thing,
A tattered coat upon a stick, unless   10
Soul clap its hands and sing, and louder sing
For every tatter in its mortal dress,
Nor is there singing school but studying
Monuments of its own magnificence;
And therefore I have sailed the seas and come   15
To the holy city of Byzantium.

O sages standing in God's holy fire
As in the gold mosaic of a wall,
Come from the holy fire, perne° in a gyre,°
And be the singing-masters of my soul.   20
Consume my heart away; sick with desire
And fastened to a dying animal
It knows not what it is; and gather me
Into the artifice of eternity.

Once out of nature I shall never take   25
My bodily form from any natural thing,
But such a form as Grecian goldsmiths make

---

19 perne descend   **gyre** spiral

Of hammered gold and gold enameling
To keep a drowsy Emperor awake;
Or set upon a golden bough to sing   30
To lords and ladies of Byzantium
Of what is past, or passing, or to come.

—1927

Edwin Arlington Robinson
1 8 6 9 – 1 9 3 5

RICHARD CORY

Whenever Richard Cory went down town,
We people on the pavement looked at him:
He was a gentleman from sole to crown,
Clean favored and imperially slim.

And he was always quietly arrayed,   5
And he was always human when he talked;
But still he fluttered pulses when he said,
"Good-morning," and he glittered when he walked.

And he was rich—yes, richer than a king—
And admirably schooled in every grace: 10
In fine, we thought that he was everything
To make us wish that we were in his place.

So on we worked, and waited for the light,
And went without the meat, and cursed the bread;
And Richard Cory, one calm summer night,   15
Went home and put a bullet through his head.

—1897

MR. FLOOD'S PARTY 🔊

Old Eben Flood, climbing alone one night
Over the hill between the town below
And the forsaken upland hermitage
That held as much as he should ever know
On earth again of home, paused warily.   5
The road was his with not a native near;
And Eben, having leisure, said aloud,
For no man else in Tilbury Town to hear:

"Well, Mr. Flood, we have the harvest moon
Again, and we may not have many more;   10
The bird is on the wing, the poet says,
And you and I have said it here before.
Drink to the bird." He raised up to the light
The jug that he had gone so far to fill,
And answered huskily: "Well, Mr. Flood,   15
Since you propose it, I believe I will."

Alone, as if enduring to the end
A valiant armor of scarred hopes outworn,
He stood there in the middle of the road
Like Roland's° ghost winding a silent horn.   20
Below him, in the town among the trees,
Where friends of other days had honored him,
A phantom salutation of the dead
Rang thinly till old Eben's eyes were dim.

Then, as a mother lays her sleeping child   25
Down tenderly, fearing it may awake,
He set the jug down slowly at his feet
With trembling care, knowing that most things break;
And only when assured that on firm earth
It stood, as the uncertain lives of men   30
Assuredly did not, he paced away,
And with his hand extended paused again:

"Well, Mr. Flood, we have not met like this
In a long time; and many a change has come
To both of us, I fear, since last it was   35
We had a drop together. Welcome home!"
Convivially returning with himself,
Again he raised the jug up to the light;

---

20 **Roland** hero of the *Chanson de Roland,* a medieval French romance

And with an acquiescent quaver said:
"Well, Mr. Flood, if you insist, I might.   40

"Only a very little, Mr. Flood—
For auld lang syne. No more, sir; that will do."
So, for the time, apparently it did,
And Eben evidently thought so too;
For soon amid the silver loneliness   45
Of night he lifted up his voice and sang,
Secure, with only two moons listening,
Until the whole harmonious landscape rang—

"For auld lang syne." The weary throat gave out,
The last word wavered; and the song being done,   50
He raised again the jug regretfully
And shook his head, and was again alone.
There was not much that was ahead of him,
And there was nothing in the town below—
Where strangers would have shut the many doors   55
That many friends had opened long ago.

    —1921

Paul Laurence Dunbar
1872–1906

WE WEAR THE MASK

We wear the mask that grins and lies,
It hides our cheeks and shades our eyes,—
This debt we pay to human guile;
With torn and bleeding hearts we smile,
And mouth with myriad subtleties.   5

Why should the world be over-wise,
In counting all our tears and sighs?
Nay, let them only see us, while
    We wear the mask.

We smile, but, O great Christ, our cries   10
To thee from tortured souls arise.
We sing, but oh the clay is vile
Beneath our feet, and long the mile;
But let the world dream otherwise,
          We wear the mask!   15

—1896

Robert Frost
1874–1963

MENDING WALL

Something there is that doesn't love a wall,
That sends the frozen-ground-swell under it,
And spills the upper boulders in the sun;
And makes gaps even two can pass abreast.
The work of hunters is another thing: 5
I have come after them and made repair
Where they have left not one stone on a stone,
But they would have the rabbit out of hiding,
To please the yelping dogs. The gaps I mean,
No one has seen them made or heard them made,   10
But at spring mending-time we find them there.
I let my neighbor know beyond the hill;
And on a day we meet to walk the line
And set the wall between us once again.
We keep the wall between us as we go.   15
To each the boulders that have fallen to each.
And some are loaves and some so nearly balls
We have to use a spell to make them balance:
"Stay where you are until our backs are turned!"
We wear our fingers rough with handling them.   20
Oh, just another kind of outdoor game,
One on a side. It comes to little more:
There where it is we do not need the wall:
He is all pine and I am apple orchard.

My apple trees will never get across   25
And eat the cones under his pines, I tell him.
He only says, "Good fences make good neighbors."
Spring is the mischief in me, and I wonder
If I could put a notion in his head:
"*Why* do they make good neighbors? Isn't it   30
Where there are cows? But here there are no cows.
Before I built a wall I'd ask to know
What I was walling in or walling out,
And to whom I was like to give offense.
Something there is that doesn't love a wall,   35
That wants it down." I could say "Elves" to him,
But it's not elves exactly, and I'd rather
He said it for himself. I see him there
Bringing a stone grasped firmly by the top
In each hand, like an old-stone savage armed.   40
He moves in darkness as it seems to me,
Not of woods only and the shade of trees.
He will not go behind his father's saying,
And he likes having thought of it so well
He says again, "Good fences make good neighbors."   45

    —1914

AFTER APPLE-PICKING

My long two-pointed ladder's sticking through a tree
Toward heaven still,
And there's a barrel that I didn't fill
Beside it, and there may be two or three
Apples I didn't pick upon some bough.   5
But I am done with apple-picking now.
Essence of winter sleep is on the night,
The scent of apples: I am drowsing off.
I cannot rub the strangeness from my sight
I got from looking through a pane of glass   10
I skimmed this morning from the drinking trough
And held against the world of hoary grass.
It melted, and I let it fall and break.
But I was well
Upon my way to sleep before it fell,   15
And I could tell
What form my dreaming was about to take.
Magnified apples appear and disappear,
Stem end and blossom end,

And every fleck of russet showing clear.   20
My instep arch not only keeps the ache,
It keeps the pressure of a ladder-round.
I feel the ladder sway as the boughs bend.
And I keep hearing from the cellar bin
The rumbling sound   25
Of load on load of apples coming in.
For I have had too much
Of apple-picking: I am overtired
Of the great harvest I myself desired.
There were ten thousand thousand fruit to touch,   30
Cherish in hand, lift down, and not let fall.
For all
That struck the earth,
No matter if not bruised or spiked with stubble,
Went surely to the cider-apple heap   35
As of no worth.
One can see what will trouble
This sleep of mine, whatever sleep it is.
Were he not gone,
The woodchuck could say whether it's like his   40
Long sleep, as I describe its coming on,
Or just some human sleep.

    —1914

BIRCHES

When I see birches bend to left and right
Across the lines of straighter darker trees,
I like to think some boy's been swinging them.
But swinging doesn't bend them down to stay
As ice storms do. Often you must have seen them   5
Loaded with ice a sunny winter morning
After a rain. They click upon themselves
As the breeze rises, and turn many-colored
As the stir cracks and crazes their enamel.
Soon the sun's warmth makes them shed crystal shells   10
Shattering and avalanching on the snow crust—
Such heaps of broken glass to sweep away
You'd think the inner dome of heaven had fallen.
They are dragged to the withered bracken by the load,
And they seem not to break; though once they are bowed   15
So low for long, they never right themselves:
You may see their trunks arching in the woods

Years afterwards, trailing their leaves on the ground
Like girls on hands and knees that throw their hair
Before them over their heads to dry in the sun.   20
But I was going to say when Truth broke in
With all her matter of fact about the ice storm
I should prefer to have some boy bend them
As he went out and in to fetch the cows—
Some boy too far from town to learn baseball,   25
Whose only play was what he found himself,
Summer or winter, and could play alone.
One by one he subdued his father's trees
By riding them down over and over again
Until he took the stiffness out of them,   30
And not one but hung limp, not one was left
For him to conquer. He learned all there was
To learn about not launching out too soon
And so not carrying the tree away
Clear to the ground. He always kept his poise   35
To the top branches, climbing carefully
With the same pains you use to fill a cup
Up to the brim, and even above the brim.
Then he flung outward, feet first, with a swish,
Kicking his way down through the air to the ground.   40
So was I once myself a swinger of birches.
And so I dream of going back to be.
It's when I'm weary of considerations,
And life is too much like a pathless wood
Where your face burns and tickles with the cobwebs   45
Broken across it, and one eye is weeping
From a twig's having lashed across it open.
I'd like to get away from earth awhile
And then come back to it and begin over.
May no fate willfully misunderstand me   50
And half grant what I wish and snatch me away
Not to return. Earth's the right place for love:
I don't know where it's likely to go better.
I'd like to go by climbing a birch tree,
And climb black branches up a snow-white trunk   55
Toward heaven, till the tree could bear no more,
But dipped its top and set me down again.
That would be good both going and coming back.
One could do worse than be a swinger of birches.

—1916

STOPPING BY WOODS
ON A SNOWY EVENING

Whose woods these are I think I know.
His house is in the village though;
He will not see me stopping here
To watch his woods fill up with snow.

My little horse must think it queer   5
To stop without a farmhouse near
Between the woods and frozen lake
The darkest evening of the year.

He gives his harness bells a shake
To ask if there is some mistake.   10
The only other sound's the sweep
Of easy wind and downy flake.

The woods are lovely, dark and deep,
But I have promises to keep,
And miles to go before I sleep,   15
And miles to go before I sleep.

    —1923

Amy Lowell
1874 – 1925

PATTERNS ▣

I walk down the garden paths,
And all the daffodils
Are blowing, and the bright blue squills.
I walk down the patterned garden-paths
In my stiff, brocaded gown.   5
With my powdered hair and jewelled fan,

I too am a rare
Pattern. As I wander down
The garden paths.

My dress is richly figured,   10
And the train
Makes a pink and silver stain
On the gravel, and the thrift
Of the borders.
Just a plate of current fashion   15
Tripping by in high-heeled, ribboned shoes.
Not a softness anywhere about me,
Only whalebone and brocade.
And I sink on a seat in the shade
Of a lime tree. For my passion   20
Wars against the stiff brocade.
The daffodils and squills
Flutter in the breeze
As they please.
And I weep;   25
For the lime-tree is in blossom
And one small flower has dropped upon my bosom.

And the plashing of waterdrops
In the marble fountain
Comes down the garden-paths.   30
The dripping never stops.
Underneath my stiffened gown
Is the softness of a woman bathing in a marble basin,
A basin in the midst of hedges grown
So thick, she cannot see her lover hiding,   35
But she guesses he is near,
And the sliding of the water
Seems the stroking of a dear
Hand upon her.
What is Summer in a fine brocaded gown!   40
I should like to see it lying in a heap upon the ground.
All the pink and silver crumpled up on the ground.

I would be the pink and silver as I ran along the paths,
And he would stumble after,
Bewildered by my laughter.   45
I should see the sun flashing from his sword-hilt and buckles on his
    shoes.
I would choose
To lead him in a maze along the patterned paths,
A bright and laughing maze for my heavy-booted lover.

Till he caught me in the shade, 50
And the buttons of his waistcoat bruised my body as he clasped me,
Aching, melting, unafraid.
With the shadows of the leaves and the sundrops,
And the plopping of the waterdrops,
All about us in the open afternoon— 55
I am very like to swoon
With the weight of this brocade,
For the sun sifts through the shade.

Underneath the fallen blossom
In my bosom, 60
Is a letter I have hid.
It was brought to me this morning by a rider from the Duke.
"Madam, we regret to inform you that Lord Hartwell
Died in action Thursday se'nnight."
As I read it in the white, morning sunlight, 65
The letters squirmed like snakes.
"Any answer, Madam," said my footman.
"No," I told him.
"See that the messenger takes some refreshment.
No, no answer." 70
And I walked into the garden,
Up and down the patterned paths,
In my stiff, correct brocade.
The blue and yellow flowers stood up proudly in the sun,
Each one. 75
I stood upright too,
Held rigid to the pattern
By the stiffness of my gown.
Up and down I walked.
Up and down. 80

In a month he would have been my husband.
In a month, here, underneath this lime,
We would have broken the pattern;
He for me, and I for him,
He as Colonel, I as Lady, 85
On this shady seat.
He had a whim
That sunlight carried blessing.
And I answered, "It shall be as you have said."
Now he is dead. 90

In Summer and In Winter I shall walk
Up and down
The patterned garden-paths

In my stiff, brocaded gown.
The squills and daffodils   95
Will give peace to pillared roses, and to asters, and to snow.
I shall go
Up and down,
In my gown.
Gorgeously arrayed,   100
Boned and stayed.
And the softness of my body will be guarded from embrace
By each button, hook, and lace.
For the man who should loose me is dead,
Fighting with the Duke in Flanders,   105
In a pattern called a war.
Christ! What are patterns for?

  —1916

Carl Sandburg
1878 – 1967

FOG

The fog comes
on little cat feet.

It sits looking
over harbor and city
on silent haunches   5
and then moves on.

  —1916

A FENCE

Now the stone house on the lake front is finished and the workmen
    are beginning the fence.
The palings are made of iron bars with steel points that can stab the
    life out of any man who falls on them.
As a fence, it is a masterpiece, and will shut off the rabble and all
    vagabonds and hungry men and all wandering children looking for
    a place to play.
Passing through the bars and over the steel points will go nothing
    except Death and the Rain and To-morrow.

    —1916

Wallace Stevens
1879–1955

THIRTEEN WAYS OF LOOKING AT A BLACKBIRD

I

Among twenty snowy mountains,
The only moving thing
Was the eye of the blackbird.

II

I was of three minds,
Like a tree
In which there are three blackbirds.

5

III

The blackbird whirled in the autumn winds.
It was a small part of the pantomime.

IV

A man and a woman
Are one.   10
A man and a woman and a blackbird
Are one.

V

I do not know which to prefer,
the beauty of inflections
Or the beauty of innuendoes,   15
The blackbird whistling
Or just after.

VI

Icicles filled the long window
With barbaric glass.
The shadow of the blackbird   20
Crossed it, to and fro.
The mood
Traced in the shadow
An indecipherable cause.

VII

O thin men of Haddam,   25
Why do you imagine golden birds?
Do you not see how the blackbird
Walks around the feet
Of the women about you?

VIII

I know noble accents   30
And lucid, inescapable rhythms;
But I know, too,
That the blackbird is involved
In what I know.

IX

When the blackbird flew out of sight,   35
It marked the edge
Of one of many circles.

X

At the sight of blackbirds
Flying in a green light,
Even the bawds of euphony   40
Would cry out sharply.

XI

He rode over Connecticut
In a glass coach.
Once, a fear pierced him,
In that he mistook   45
The shadow of his equipage
For blackbirds.

XII

The river is moving.
The blackbird must be flying.

XIII

It was evening all afternoon.   50
It was snowing
And it was going to snow.
The blackbird sat
In the cedar-limbs.

—1917

THE SNOW MAN

One must have a mind of winter
To regard the frost and the boughs
Of the pine-trees crusted with snow;

And have been cold a long time
To behold the junipers shagged with ice,   5
The spruces rough in the distant glitter

Of the January sun; and not to think
Of any misery in the sound of the wind,
In the sound of a few leaves,

Which is the sound of the land   10
Full of the same wind
That is blowing in the same bare place

For the listener, who listens in the snow,
And, nothing himself, beholds
Nothing that is not there and the nothing that is.   15

   —1921

THE EMPEROR OF ICE-CREAM

Call the roller of big cigars,
The muscular one, and bid him whip
In kitchen cups concupiscent curds.
Let the wenches dawdle in such dress
As they are used to wear, and let the boys   5
Bring flowers in last month's newspapers.
Let be be finale of seem.
The only emperor is the emperor of ice-cream.

Take from the dresser of deal,
Lacking the three glass knobs, that sheet   10
On which she embroidered fantails once
And spread it so as to cover her face.
If her horny feet protrude, they come
To show how cold she is, and dumb.
Let the lamp affix its beam.   15
The only emperor is the emperor of ice-cream.

   —1922

William Carlos Williams
1883–1963

TO WAKEN AN OLD LADY

Old age is
a flight of small
cheeping birds
skimming
bare trees   5
above a snow glaze.
Gaining and failing
they are buffeted
by a dark wind—
But what?   10
On harsh weedstalks
the flock has rested—
the snow
is covered with broken
seed husks   15
and the wind tempered
with a shrill
piping of plenty.
        —1920

THE RED WHEELBARROW

so much depends
upon

a red wheel
barrow

glazed with rain   5
water

beside the white
chickens
        —1923

THIS IS JUST TO SAY

I have eaten
the plums
that were in
the icebox
and which   5
you were probably
saving
for breakfast

Forgive me
they were delicious   10
so sweet
and so cold

    —1934

Elinor Wylie
1885 – 1928

WILD PEACHES 𝕹

I

When the world turns completely upside down
You say we'll emigrate to the Eastern Shore
Aboard a river-boat from Baltimore;
We'll live among wild peach trees, miles from town,
You'll wear a coonskin cap, and I a gown   5
Homespun, dyed butternut's dark gold colour.
Lost, like your lotus-eating ancestor,
We'll swim in milk and honey till we drown.

The winter will be short, the summer long,
The autumn amber-hued, sunny and hot,   10
Tasting of cider and of scuppernong;
All seasons sweet, but autumn best of all.
The squirrels in their silver fur will fall
Like falling leaves, like fruit, before your shot.

2

The autumn frosts will lie upon the grass   15
Like bloom on grapes of purple-brown and gold.
The misted early mornings will be cold;
The little puddles will be roofed with glass.
The sun, which burns from copper into brass,
Melts these at noon, and makes the boys unfold   20
Their knitted mufflers; full as they can hold,
Fat pockets dribble chestnuts as they pass.

Peaches grow wild, and pigs can live in clover;
A barrel of salted herrings lasts a year;
The spring begins before the winter's over.   25
By February you may find the skins
Of garter snakes and water moccasins
Dwindled and harsh, dead-white and cloudy-clear.

3

When April pours the colours of a shell
Upon the hills, when every little creek   30
Is shot with silver from the Chesapeake
In shoals new-minted by the ocean swell,
When strawberries go begging, and the sleek
Blue plums lie open to the blackbird's beak,
We shall live well—we shall live very well.   35

The months between the cherries and the peaches
Are brimming cornucopias which spill
Fruits red and purple, sombre-bloomed and black;
Then, down rich fields and frosty river beaches
We'll trample bright persimmons, while you kill   40
Bronze patridge, speckled quail, and canvasback.

4

Down to the Puritan marrow of my bones
There's something in this richness that I hate.
I love the look, austere, immaculate,
Of landscapes drawn in pearly monotones.   45
There's something in my very blood that owns
Bare hills, cold silver on a sky of slate,
A thread of water, churned to milky spate
Streaming through slanted pastures fenced with stones.

I love those skies, thin blue or snowy gray,   50
Those fields sparse-planted, rendering meagre sheaves;
That spring, briefer than apple-blossom's breath,
Summer, so much too beautiful to stay,
Swift autumn, like a bonfire of leaves,
And sleepy winter, like the sleep of death.   55

    —1921

Ezra Pound
1 8 8 5 – 1 9 7 2

THE RIVER-MERCHANT'S WIFE: A LETTER°

While my hair was still cut straight across my forehead
Played I about the front gate, pulling flowers.
You came by on bamboo stilts, playing horse,
You walked about my seat, playing with blue plums.
And we went on living in the village of Chōkan: 5
Two small people, without dislike or suspicion.

At fourteen I married My Lord you.
I never laughed, being bashful.

Pound translated and adapted this poem from Chinese poet Li T'ai Po.

Lowering my head, I looked at the wall.
Called to, a thousand times, I never looked back.   10

At fifteen I stopped scowling,
I desired my dust to be mingled with yours
Forever and forever and forever.
Why should I climb the look out?

At sixteen you departed,   15
You went into far Ku-tō-en, by the river of swirling eddies,
And you have been gone five months.
The monkeys make sorrowful noise overhead.

You dragged your feet when you went out.
By the gate now, the moss is grown, the different mosses,   20
Too deep to clear them away!
The leaves fall early this autumn, in wind.
The paired butterflies are already yellow with August

Over the grass in the West garden;
They hurt me. I grow older.   25
If you are coming down through the narrows of the river Kiang,
Please let me know before hand,
And I will come out to meet you
                     As far as Chō-fū-Sa.

        1915

IN A STATION OF THE METRO

The apparition of these faces in the crowd;
    Petals on a wet, black bough.

        —1916

H. D. (Hilda Doolittle)
1886–1961

HEAT

O wind, rend open the heat,
cut apart the heat,
rend it to tatters.

Fruit cannot drop
through this thick air—   5
fruit cannot fall into heat
that presses up and blunts
the points of pears
and rounds the grapes.

Cut the heat—   10
plough through it,
turning it on either side
of your path.

—1916

Marianne Moore
1887–1972

POETRY

I, too, dislike it: there are things that are important beyond all
   this fiddle.
   Reading it, however, with a perfect contempt for it, one
      discovers in
   it after all, a place for the genuine.
      Hands that can grasp, eyes
         that can dilate, hair that can rise   5
            if it must, these things are important not because a

high-sounding interpretation can be put upon them but because they are
    useful. When they become so derivative as to become unintelliglble,
    the same thing may be said for all of us, that we
        do not admire what   10
        we cannot understand: the bat
            holding on upside down or in quest of something to

eat, elephants pushing, a wild horse taking a roll, a tireless wolf under
    a tree, the immovable critic twitching his skin like a horse that
    feels a
        flea, the base-   15
    ball fan, the statistician—
        nor is it valid
            to discriminate against "business documents and

school-books"°; all these phenomena are important. One must make a
    distinction however: when dragged into prominence by half poets,
    the result is
        not poetry,
    nor till the poets among us can be   20
        "literalists of
        the imagination"°—above
        insolence and triviality and can present

for inspection, "imaginary gardens with real toads in them," shall
    we have
    it. In the meantime, if you demand on the one hand,   25
    the raw material of poetry in
        all its rawness and
        that which is on the other hand
            genuine, you are interested in poetry.

    —1921

---

19 *"Diary of Tolstoy* (Dutton), p. 84. 'Where the boundary between prose and poetry lies, I shall never be able to understand. The question is raised in manuals of style, yet the answer lies beyond me. Poetry is verse; prose is not verse. Or else poetry is everything with the exception of business documents and school books.'" [Moore's note]

22 *"Yeats: Ideas of Good and Evil* (A. H. Bullen), p. 182. 'The limitation of his view was from the very intensity of his vision; he was a too literal realist of the imagination, as others are of nature; and because he believed that the figures seen by the mind's eye, when exhalted by inspiration, were 'external existences,' symbols of divine essences, he hated every grace of style that might obscure their lineaments.'" [Moore's note. Yeats refers to William Blake.]

A GRAVE°

Man looking into the sea,
taking the view from those who have as much right to it as you have
    to it yourself,
it is human nature to stand in the middle of a thing,
but you cannot stand in the middle of this;
the sea has nothing to give but a well excavated grave.   5
The firs stand in a procession, each with an emerald turkey foot at
    the top,
reserved as their contours, saying nothing;
repression, however, is not the most obvious characteristic of the sea;
the sea is a collector, quick to return a rapacious look.
There are others besides you who have worn that look—   10
whose expression is no longer a protest; the fish no longer investigate
    them
for their bones have not lasted:
men lower nets, unconscious of the fact that they are desecrating a
    grave,
and row quickly away—the blades of the oars
moving together like the feet of water spiders as if there were no   15
    such thing as death.
The wrinkles progress among themselves in a phalanx—beautiful
    under networks of foam,
and fade breathlessly while the sea rustles in and out of the
    seaweed;
the birds swim through the air at top speed, emitting catcalls as
    heretofore—
the tortoise shell scourges about the feet of the cliffs, in motion
    beneath them;
and the ocean, under the pulsation of lighthouses and noise of bell   20
    buoys,
advances as usual, looking as if it were not that ocean in which
    dropped things are bound to sink—
in which if they turn and twist, it is neither with volition nor
    consciousness.

    —1921

Originally published as "A Graveyard."

T. S. Eliot
1 8 8 8 – 1 9 6 5

THE LOVE SONG OF
J. ALFRED PRUFROCK

S'io credesse che mia risposta fosse
A persona che mai tornasse al mondo,
Questa fiamma staria senza più scosse.
Ma perciocche giammai di questo fondo
Non tornò vivo alcun, s'i'odo il vero,
Senza tema d'infamia ti rispondo.°

Let us go then, you and I,
When the evening is spread out against the sky
Like a patient etherised upon a table;
Let us go, through certain half-deserted streets,
The muttering retreats   5
Of restless nights in one-night cheap hotels
And sawdust restaurants with oyster-shells:
Streets that follow like a tedious argument
Of insidious intent
To lead you to an overwhelming question . . .   10
Oh, do not ask, "What is it?"
Let us go and make our visit.

In the room the women come and go
Talking of Michelangelo.

The yellow fog that rubs its back upon the window-panes   15
The yellow smoke that rubs its muzzle on the window-panes
Licked its tongue into the corners of the evening,
Lingered upon the pools that stand in drains,
Let fall upon its back the soot that falls from chimneys,
Slipped by the terrace, made a sudden leap,   20
And seeing that it was a soft October night,
Curled once about the house, and fell asleep.

---

rispondo Guido da Montefeltro speaking in Dante's *Inferno,* canto XXVII, 61–66: "If I believed that my reply were made / To one who to the world would e'er return, / This flame without more flickering would stand still; / But inasmuch as never from this depth / Did anyone return, if I hear true, / without the fear of infamy I answer." (Transl. H. W. Longfellow.)

And indeed there will be time
For the yellow smoke that slides along the street,
Rubbing its back upon the window-panes;   25
There will be time, there will be time
To prepare a face to meet the faces that you meet;
There will be time to murder and create,
And time for all the works and days of hands
That lift and drop a question on your plate;   30
Time for you and time for me,
And time yet for a hundred indecisions,
And for a hundred visions and revisions,
Before the taking of a toast and tea.

In the room the women come and go   35
Talking of Michelangelo.

And indeed there will be time
To wonder, "Do I dare?" and, "Do I dare?"
Time to turn back and descend the stair,
With a bald spot in the middle of my hair—   40
(They will say: "How his hair is growing thin!")
My morning coat, my collar mounting firmly to the chin,
My necktie rich and modest, but asserted by a simple pin—
(They will say: "But how his arms and legs are thin!")
Do I dare   45
Disturb the universe?
In a minute there is time
For decisions and revisions which a minute will reverse.

For I have known them all already, known them all:
Have known the evenings, mornings, afternoons,   50
I have measured out my life with coffee spoons;
I know the voices dying with a dying fall
Beneath the music from a farther room.
    So how should I presume?

And I have known the eyes already, known them all—   55
The eyes that fix you in a formulated phrase,
And when I am formulated, sprawling on a pin,
When I am pinned and wriggling on the wall,
Then how should I begin
To spit out all the butt-ends of my days and ways?   60
    And how should I presume?

And I have known the arms already, known them all—
Arms that are braceleted and white and bare
(But in the lamplight, downed with light brown hair!)

Is it perfume from a dress   65
That makes me so digress?
Arms that lie along a table, or wrap about a shawl.
   And should I then presume?
   And how should I begin?

                  . . . . .

Shall I say, I have gone at dusk through narrow streets   70
And watched the smoke that rises from the pipes
Of lonely men in shirt-sleeves, leaning out of windows? . . .

I should have been a pair of ragged claws
Scuttling across the floors of silent seas.

                  . . . . .

And the afternoon, the evening, sleeps so peacefully!   75
Smoothed by long fingers,
Asleep . . . tired . . . or it malingers,
Stretched on the floor, here beside you and me.
Should I, after tea and cakes and ices,
Have the strength to force the moment to its crisis?   80
But though I have wept and fasted, wept and prayed,
Though I have seen my head (grown slightly bald) brought in
   upon a platter,
I am no prophet—and here's no great matter;
I have seen the moment of my greatness flicker,
And I have seen the eternal Footman hold my coat, and snicker,   85
And in short, I was afraid.

And would it have been worth it, after all,
After the cups, the marmalade, the tea,
Among the porcelain, among some talk of you and me,
Would it have been worth while,   90
To have bitten off the matter with a smile,
To have squeezed the universe into a ball
To roll it toward some overwhelming question,
To say: "I am Lazarus, come from the dead,
Come back to tell you all, I shall tell you all"—   95
If one, settling a pillow by her head,
   Should say: "That is not what I meant at all.
   That is not it, at all."

And would it have been worth it, after all,
Would it have been worth while,   100
After the sunsets and the dooryards and the sprinkled streets,
After the novels, after the teacups, after the skirts that trail along
    the floor—
And this, and so much more?—
It is impossible to say just what I mean!
But as if a magic lantern threw the nerves in patterns on
    a screen: 105
Would it have been worth while
If one, settling a pillow or throwing off a shawl,
And turning toward the window, should say:
    "That is not it at all,
    That is not what I meant, at all."   110

                    .   .   .   .   .

No! I am not Prince Hamlet, nor was meant to be;
Am an attendant lord, one that will do
To swell a progress, start a scene or two,
Advise the prince; no doubt, an easy tool,
Deferential, glad to be of use,   115
Politic, cautious, and meticulous;
Full of high sentence, but a bit obtuse;
At times, indeed, almost ridiculous—
Almost, at times, the Fool.

I grow old . . . I grow old . . .   120
I shall wear the bottoms of my trousers rolled.

Shall I part my hair behind? Do I dare to eat a peach?
I shall wear white flannel trousers, and walk upon the beach.
I have heard the mermaids singing, each to each.

I do not think that they will sing to me.   125

I have seen them riding seaward on the waves
Combing the white hair of the waves blown back
When the wind blows the water white and black.

We have lingered in the chambers of the sea
By sea-girls wreathed with seaweed red and brown   130
Till human voices wake us, and we drown.

        —1917

PRELUDES

I

The winter evening settles down
With smell of steaks in passageways.
Six o'clock.
The burnt-out ends of smoky days.
And now a gusty shower wraps   5
The grimy scraps
Of withered leaves about your feet
And newspapers from vacant lots;
The showers beat
On broken blinds and chimney-pots,   10
And at the corner of the street
A lonely cab-horse steams and stamps.
And then the lighting of the lamps.

II

The morning comes to consciousness
Of faint stale smells of beer   15
From the sawdust-trampled street
With all its muddy feet that press
To early coffee-stands.
With the other masquerades
That time resumes,   20
One thinks of all the hands
That are raising dingy shades
In a thousand furnished rooms.

III

You tossed a blanket from the bed,
You lay upon your back, and waited;   25
You dozed, and watched the night revealing
The thousand sordid images
Of which your soul was constituted;
They flickered against the ceiling.
And when all the world came back   30
And the light crept up between the shutters

And you heard the sparrows in the gutters,
You had such a vision of the street
As the street hardly understands;
Sitting along the bed's edge, where   35
You curled the papers from your hair,
Or clasped the yellow soles of feet
In the palms of both soiled hands.

IV

His soul stretched tight across the skies
That fade behind a city block,   40
Or trampled by insistent feet
At four and five and six o'clock;
And short square fingers stuffing pipes,
And evening newspapers, and eyes
Assured of certain certainties,   45
The conscience of a blackened street
Impatient to assume the world.
    I am moved by fancies that are curled
Around these images, and cling:
The notion of some infinitely gentle   50
Infinitely suffering thing.

    Wipe your hand across your mouth, and laugh;
The worlds revolve like ancient women
Gathering fuel in vacant lots.
    —1917

John Crowe Ransom
1888–1974

BELLS FOR JOHN WHITESIDE'S DAUGHTER

There was such speed in her little body,
And such lightness in her footfall,
It is no wonder her brown study
Astonishes us all.

Her wars were bruited in our high window.   5
We looked among orchard trees and beyond,
Where she took arms against her shadow,
Or harried unto the pond

The lazy geese, like a snow cloud
Dripping their snow on the green grass,   10
Tricking and stopping, sleepy and proud,
Who cried in goose, Alas,

For the tireless heart within the little
Lady with rod that made them rise
From their noon apple-dreams and scuttle   15
Goose-fashion under the skies!

But now go the bells, and we are ready;
In one house we are sternly stopped
To say we are vexed at her brown study,
Lying so primly propped.   20

—1924

Claude McKay
1889–1948

AMERICA ▣

Although she feeds me bread of bitterness,
And sinks into my throat her tiger's tooth,
Stealing my breath of life, I will confess
I love this cultured hell that tests my youth!
Her vigor flows like tides into my blood,   5
Giving me strength erect against her hate.
Her bigness sweeps my being like a flood.
Yet as a rebel fronts a king in state,
I stand within her walls with not a shred
Of terror, malice, not a word of jeer.   10
Darkly I gaze into the days ahead,
And see her might and granite wonders there,
Beneath the touch of Time's unerring hand,
Like priceless treasures sinking in the sand.

—1921

Edna St. Vincent Millay
1892–1950

FIRST FIG ▣

My candle burns at both ends;
    It will not last the night;
But ah, my foes, and oh, my friends—
    It gives a lovely light!

—1920

WHAT LIPS MY LIPS HAVE KISSED, AND WHERE, AND WHY

What lips my lips have kissed, and where, and why,
I have forgotten, and what arms have lain
Under my head till morning; but the rain
Is full of ghosts tonight, that tap and sigh
Upon the glass and listen for reply,   5
And in my heart there stirs a quiet pain
For unremembered lads that not again
Will turn to me at midnight with a cry.
Thus in the winter stands the lonely tree,
Nor knows what birds have vanished one by one,   10
Yet knows its boughs more silent than before:
I cannot say what loves have come and gone,
I only know that summer sang in me
A little while, that in me sings no more.

       —1923

Archibald MacLeish
1 8 9 2 – 1 9 8 2

ARS POETICA

A poem should be palpable and mute
As a globed fruit,

Dumb
As old medallions to the thumb,

Silent as the sleeve-worn stone   5
Of casement ledges where the moss has grown—

A poem should be worldless
As the flight of birds.

A poem should be motionless in time
As the moon climbs,   10

Leaving, as the moon releases
Twig by twig the night-entangled trees,

Leaving, as the moon behind the winter leaves,
Memory by memory the mind—

A poem should be motionless in time   15
As the moon climbs.

A poem should be equal to:
Not true.

For all the history of grief
An empty doorway and a maple leaf.   20

For love
The leaning grasses and two lights above the sea—

A poem should not mean
But be.

    —1926

Wilfred Owen
1 8 9 3 – 1 9 1 8

DULCE ET DECORUM EST

Bent double, like old beggars under sacks,
Knock-kneed, coughing like hags, we cursed through sludge,
Till on the haunting flares we turned our backs
And towards our distant rest began to trudge.
Men marched asleep. Many had lost their boots,   5
But limped on, blood-shod. All went lame, all blind;

Drunk with fatigue; deaf even to the hoots
Of gas-shells dropping softly behind.

Gas! GAS! Quick, boys!—An ecstasy of fumbling,
Fitting the clumsy helmets just in time,   10
But someone still was yelling out and stumbling
And flound'ring like a man in fire or lime. —
Dim through the misty panes and thick green light,
As under a green sea, I saw him drowning.

In all my dreams before my helpless sight   15
He plunges at me, guttering, choking, drowning.

If in some smothering dreams, you too could pace
Behind the wagon that we flung him in,
And watch the white eyes writhing in his face,
His hanging face, like a devil's sick of sin,   20
If you could hear, at every jolt, the blood
Come gargling from the froth-corrupted lungs,
Bitter as the cud
Of vile, incurable sores on innocent tongues,—
My friend, you would not tell with such high zest   25
To children ardent for some desperate glory,
The old Lie: *Dulce et decorum est*
Pro patria mori.°

        —1920

27–28 *Dulce et decorum est pro patria mori* "It is sweet and fitting to die for one's country." From an ode by Roman poet Horace.

Dorothy Parker
1893–1967

RÉSUMÉ

Razors pain you;
Rivers are damp;
Acids stain you;
And drugs cause cramp.
Guns aren't lawful;   5
Nooses give;
Gas smells awful;
You might as well live.

    —1926

E. E. Cummings
1894–1962

BUFFALO BILL'S

Buffalo Bill's
defunct
    who used to
    ride a watersmooth-silver
                stallion   5
and break onetwothreefourfive pigeonsjustlikethat
                       Jesus
he was a handsome man
            and what i want to know is
how do you like your blueeyed boy   10
Mister Death

    —1920

IN JUST-

in Just-
spring   when the world is mud-
luscious the little
lame balloonman

whistles   far   and wee   5

and eddieandbill come
running from marbles and
piracies and it's
spring

when the world is puddle-wonderful   10
the queer
old balloonman whistles
far   and   wee
and bettyandisbel come dancing

from hop-scotch and jump-rope and   15

it's
spring
and
     the

          goat-footed   20

balloonMan   whistles
far
and
wee
     —1923

ANYONE LIVED IN A PRETTY HOW TOWN

anyone lived in a pretty how town
(with up so floating many bells down)
spring summer autumn winter
he sang his didn't he danced his did.

Women and men (both little and small)   5
cared for anyone not at all
they sowed their isn't they reaped their same
sun moon stars rain

children guessed (but only a few
and down they forgot as up they grew   10
autumn winter spring summer)
that noone loved him more by more

when by now and tree by leaf
she laughed his joy she cried his grief
bird by snow and stir by still   15
anyone's any was all to her

someones married their everyones
laughed their cryings and did their dance
(sleep wake hope and then) they
said their nevers they slept their dream   20

stars rain sun moon
(and only the snow can begin to explain
how children are apt to forget to remember
with up so floating many bells down)

one day anyone died i guess   25
(and noone stooped to kiss his face)
busy folk buried them side by side
little by little and was by was

all by all and deep by deep
and more by more they dream their sleep   30
noone and anyone earth by april
wish by spirit and if by yes.

Women and men (both dong and ding)
summer autumn winter spring
reaped their sowing and went their came   35
sun moon stars rain

—1940

Jean Toomer
1894–1967

SONG OF THE SON

Pour, O pour, that parting soul in song,
O pour it in the saw-dust glow of night,
Into the velvet pine-smoke air tonight,
And let the valley carry it along,
And let the valley carry it along.   5

O land and soil, red soil and sweet-gum tree
So scant of grass, so profligate of pines,
Now just before an epoch's sun declines
Thy son, in time, I have returned to thee,
Thy son, I have in time returned to thee.   10

In time, for though the sun is setting on
A song-lit race of slaves, it has not set;
Though late, O soil it is not too late yet
To catch thy plaintive soul, leaving, soon gone,
Leaving, to catch thy plaintive soul soon gone.   15

O Negro slaves, dark-purple ripened plums,
Squeezed, and bursting in the pine-wood air,
Passing, before they stripped the old tree bare
One plum was saved for me, one seed becomes

An everlasting song, a singing tree,   20
Carolling softly souls of slavery,
All that they were, and that they are to me,—
Carolling softly souls of slavery.

        —1922

REAPERS

Black reapers with the sound of steel on stones
Are sharpening scythes. I see them place the hones
In their hip-pockets as a thing that's done,
And start their silent swinging, one by one.
Black horses drive a mower through the weeds,   5
And there, a field rat, startled, squealing bleeds,
His belly close to ground. I see the blade,
Blood-stained, continue cutting weeds and shade.

   —1923

Langston Hughes
1902–1967

THE NEGRO SPEAKS OF RIVERS

I've known rivers:
I've known rivers ancient as the world and older than the flow of
   human blood in human veins.

My soul has grown deep like the rivers.

I bathed in the Euphrates when dawns were young.
I built my hut near the Congo and it lulled me to sleep.   5
I looked upon the Nile and raised the pyramids above it.
I heard the singing of the Mississippi when Abe Lincoln went
    down to New Orleans, and I've seen its muddy bosom turn
    all golden in the sunset.

I've known rivers:
Ancient, dusky rivers.

My soul has grown deep like the rivers.   10

   —1921

MOTHER TO SON

Well, son, I'll tell you:
Life for me ain't been no crystal stair.
It's had tacks in it,
And splinters,
And boards torn up,   5
And places with no carpet on the floor—
Bare.
But all the time
I'se been a-climbin' on,
And reachin' landin's,   10
And turnin' corners,
And sometimes goin' in the dark
Where there ain't been no light.
So boy, don't you turn back.
Don't you set down on the steps   15
'Cause you finds it's kinder hard.
Don't you fall now—
For I'se still goin', honey,
I'se still climbin',
And life for me ain't been no crystal stair.   20

    —1922

HARLEM

What happens to a dream deferred?

    Does it dry up
    like a raisin in the sun?
    Or fester like a sore—
    And then run?   5
    Does it stink like rotten meat?
    Or crust and sugar over—
    like a syrupy sweet?

    Maybe it just sags
    like a heavy load.   10

    Or does it explode?

    —1951

Countee Cullen
1903–1946

INCIDENT

Once riding in old Baltimore,
   Heart-filled, head-filled with glee,
I saw a Baltimorean
   Keep looking straight at me.

Now I was eight and very small,   5
   And he was no whit bigger,
And so I smiled, but he poked out
   His tongue, and called me, "Nigger."

I saw the whole of Baltimore
   From May until December;   10
Of all the things that happened there
   That's all that I remember.

     —1924

W. H. Auden
1907–1973

MUSÉE DES BEAUX ARTS

About suffering they were never wrong,
The Old Masters: how well they understood
Its human position; how it takes place
While someone else is eating or opening a window or just walking
   dully along
How, when the aged are reverently, passionately waiting   5
For the miraculous birth, there always must be

Children who did not specially want it to happen, skating
On a pond at the edge of the wood:
They never forgot
That even the dreadful martyrdom must run its course   10
Anyhow in a corner, some untidy spot
Where the dogs go on with their doggy life and the torturer's horse
Scratches its innocent behind on a tree.
In Brueghel's *Icarus,* for instance: how everything turns away
Quite leisurely from the disaster; the ploughman may   15
Have heard the splash, the forsaken cry,
But for him it was not an important failure; the sun shone
As it had to on the white legs disappearing into the green
Water; and the expensive delicate ship that must have seen
Something amazing, a boy falling out of the sky,   20
Had somewhere to get to and sailed calmly on.

    —1940

Theodore Roethke
1908–1963

MY PAPA'S WALTZ

The whiskey on your breath
Could make a small boy dizzy;
But I hung on like death:
Such waltzing was not easy.

We romped until the pans   5
Slid from the kitchen shelf;
My mother's countenance
Could not unfrown itself.

The hand that held my wrist
Was battered on one knuckle;   10
At every step you missed
My right ear scraped a buckle.

You beat time on my head
With a palm caked hard by dirt,
Then waltzed me off to bed   15
Still clinging to your shirt.

     1948

Elizabeth Bishop
1911–1979

THE FISH

I caught a tremendous fish
and held him beside the boat
half out of water, with my hook
fast in a corner of his mouth.
He didn't fight.   5
He hadn't fought at all.
He hung a grunting weight,
battered and venerable
and homely. Here and there
his brown skin hung in strips   10
like ancient wallpaper,
and its pattern of darker brown
was like wallpaper:
shapes like full-blown roses
stained and lost through age.   15
He was speckled with barnacles,
fine rosettes of lime,
and infested
with tiny white sea-lice,
and underneath two or three   20
rags of green weed hung down.
While his gills were breathing in
the terrible oxygen
—the frightening gills,
fresh and crisp with blood,   25
that can cut so badly—

I thought of the coarse white flesh
packed in like feathers,
the big bones and the little bones,
the dramatic reds and blacks   30
of his shiny entrails,
and the pink swim-bladder
like a big peony.
I looked into his eyes
which were far larger than mine   35
but shallower, and yellowed,
the irises backed and packed
with tarnished tinfoil
seen through the lenses
of old scratched isinglass.   40
They shifted a little, but not
to return my stare.
—It was more like the tipping
of an object toward the light.
I admired his sullen face,   45
the mechanism of his jaw,
and then I saw
that from his lower lip
—if you could call it a lip—
grim, wet, and weaponlike,   50
hung five old pieces of fish-line,
or four and a wire leader
with the swivel still attached,
with all their five big hooks
grown firmly in his mouth.   55
A green line, frayed at the end
where he broke it, two heavier lines,
and a fine black thread
still crimped from the strain and snap
when it broke and he got away.   60
Like medals with their ribbons
frayed and wavering,
a five-haired beard of wisdom
trailing from his aching jaw.
I stared and stared   65
and victory filled up
the little rented boat,
from the pool of bilge
where oil had spread a rainbow
around the rusted engine   70
to the bailer rusted orange,
the sun-cracked thwarts,
the oarlocks on their strings,

the gunnels—until everything
was rainbow, rainbow, rainbow!   75
And I let the fish go.

   —1946

SESTINA

September rain falls on the house.
In the failing light, the old grandmother
sits in the kitchen with the child
beside the Little Marvel Stove,
reading the jokes from the almanac,   5
laughing and talking to hide her tears.

She thinks that her equinoctial tears
and the rain that beats on the roof of the house
were both foretold by the almanac,
but only known to a grandmother.   10
The iron kettle sings on the stove.
She cuts some bread and says to the child,

It's time for tea now; but the child
is watching the teakettle's small hard tears
dance like mad on the hot black stove,   15
the way the rain must dance on the house.
Tidying up, the old grandmother
hangs up the clever almanac

on its string. Birdlike, the almanac
hovers half open above the child,   20
hovers above the old grandmother
and her teacup full of dark brown tears.
She shivers and says she thinks the house
feels chilly, and puts more wood in the stove.

It was to be, says the Marvel Stove.   25
I know what I know, says the almanac.
With crayons the child draws a rigid house
and a winding pathway. Then the child
puts in a man with buttons like tears
and shows it proudly to the grandmother.   30

But secretly, while the grandmother
busies herself about the stove,

the little moons fall down like tears
from between the pages of the almanac
into the flower bed the child   35
has carefully placed in the front of the house.

Time to plant tears, says the almanac.
The grandmother sings to the marvelous stove
and the child draws another inscrutable house.

    —1965

Robert Hayden
1 9 1 3 – 1 9 8 0

THOSE WINTER SUNDAYS

Sundays too my father got up early
and put his clothes on in the blueblack cold,
then with cracked hands that ached
from labor in the weekday weather made
banked fires blaze. No one ever thanked him.   5

I'd wake and hear the cold splintering, breaking.
When the rooms were warm, he'd call,
and slowly I would rise and dress,
fearing the chronic angers of that house,

Speaking indifferently to him,   10
who had driven out the cold
and polished my good shoes as well.
What did I know, what did I know
of love's austere and lonely offices?

    —1962

John Frederick Nims
1913–1999

LOVE POEM

My clumsiest dear, whose hands shipwreck vases,
At whose quick touch all glasses chip and ring,
Whose palms are bulls in china, burs in linen,
And have no cunning with any soft thing

Except all ill-at-ease fidgeting people: 5
The refugee uncertain at the door
You make at home; deftly you steady
The drunk clambering on his undulant floor.

Unpredictable dear, the taxi drivers' terror,
Shrinking from far headlights pale as a dime   10
Yet leaping before red apoplectic streetcars—
Misfit in any space. And never on time.

A wrench in clocks and the solar system. Only
With words and people and love you move at ease.
In traffic of wit expertly maneuver   15
And keep us, all devotion, at your knees.

Forgetting your coffee spreading on our flannel,
Your lipstick grinning on our coat,
So gaily in love's unbreakable heaven
Our souls on glory of spilt bourbon float.   20

Be with me, darling, early and late. Smash glasses—
I will study wry music for your sake.
For should your hands drop white and empty
All the toys of the world would break.

—1947

William Stafford
1 9 1 4 – 1 9 9 3

TRAVELING THROUGH THE DARK

Traveling through the dark I found a deer
dead on the edge of the Wilson River road.
It is usually best to roll them into the canyon:
that road is narrow; to swerve might make more dead.

By glow of the tail-light I stumbled back of the car   5
and stood by the heap, a doe, a recent killing;
she had stiffened already, almost cold.
I dragged her off; she was large in the belly.

My fingers touching her side brought me the reason—
her side was warm; her fawn lay there waiting,   10
alive, still, never to be born.
Beside that mountain road I hesitated.

The car aimed ahead its lowered parking lights;
under the hood purred the steady engine.
I stood in the glare of the warm exhaust turning red;   15
around our group I could hear the wilderness listen.

I thought hard for us all—my only swerving—,
then pushed her over the edge into the river.

—1962

Dylan Thomas
1 9 1 4 – 1 9 5 3

FERN HILL

Now as I was young and easy under the apple boughs
About the lilting house and happy as the grass was green,
  The night above the dingle° starry,
   Time let me hail and climb
  Golden in the heydays of his eyes,   5
And honored among wagons I was prince of the apple towns
And once below a time I lordly had the trees and leaves
   Trail with daisies and barley
  Down the rivers of the windfall light.

And as I was green and carefree, famous among the barns 10
About the happy yard and singing as the farm was home,
  In the sun that is young once only,
   Time let me play and be
  Golden in the mercy of his means,
And green and golden I was huntsman and herdsman, the calves 15
Sang to my horn, the foxes on the hills barked clear and cold,
   And the sabbath rang slowly
  In the pebbles of the holy streams.

All the sun long it was running, it was lovely, the hay
Fields high as the house, the tunes from the chimneys, it was air 20
  And playing, lovely and watery
   And fire green as grass.
  And nightly under the simple stars
As I rode to sleep the owls were bearing the farm away,
All the moon long I heard, blessed among stables, the nightjars 25
  Flying with the ricks, and the horses
   Flashing into the dark.

And then to awake, and the farm, like a wanderer white
With the dew, come back, the cock on his shoulder: it was all
  Shining, it was Adam and maiden,   30
   The sky gathered again
  And the sun grew round that very day.

---

3 dingle wooded valley

So it must have been after the birth of the simple light
In the first, spinning place, the spellbound horses walking warm
       Out of the whinnying green stable   35
         On to the fields of praise.

And honored among foxes and pheasants by the gay house
Under the new made clouds and happy as the heart was long,
       In the sun born over and over,
         I ran my heedless ways,   40
       My wishes raced through the house high hay
And nothing I cared, at my sky blue trades, that time allows
In all his tuneful turning so few and such morning songs
       Before the children green and golden
         Follow him out of grace,   45

Nothing I cared, in the lamb white days, that time would take me
Up to the swallow thronged loft by the shadow of my hand,
       In the moon that is always rising,
         Nor that riding to sleep
       I should hear him fly with the high fields   50
And wake to the farm forever fled from the childless land.
Oh as I was young and easy in the mercy of his means,
        Time held me green and dying
       Though I sang in my chains like the sea.

   —1946

DO NOT GO GENTLE
INTO THAT GOOD NIGHT

Do not go gentle into that good night,
Old age should burn and rave at close of day;
Rage, rage against the dying of the light.

Though wise men at their end know dark is right,
Because their words had forked no lightning they   5
Do not go gentle into that good night.

Good men, the last wave by, crying how bright
Their frail deeds might have danced in a green bay,
Rage, rage against the dying of the light.

Wild men who caught and sang the sun in flight,   10
And learn, too late, they grieved it on its way,
Do not go gentle into that good night.

Grave men, near death, who see with blinding sight
Blind eyes could blaze like meteors and be gay,
Rage, rage against the dying of the light.   15

And you, my father, there on the sad height,
Curse, bless, me now with your fierce tears, I pray.
Do not go gentle into that good night.
Rage, rage against the dying of the light.

   —1952

Randall Jarrell
1 9 1 4 – 1 9 6 5

THE DEATH OF THE
BALL TURRET GUNNER

From my mother's sleep I fell into the State
And I hunched in its belly till my wet fur froze.
Six miles from earth, loosed from its dream of life,
I woke to black flak and the nightmare fighters.
When I died they washed me out of the turret with a hose.   5

   —1945

John Berryman
1914–1972

DREAM SONG

4

Filling her compact & delicious body
with chicken páprika, she glanced at me
twice.
Fainting with interest, I hungered back
and only the fact of her husband & four other people   5
kept me from springing on her

or falling at her little feet and crying
'You are the hottest one for years of night
Henry's dazed eyes
have enjoyed, Brilliance.' I advanced upon   10
(despairing) my spumoni.—Sir Bones: is stuffed,
de world, wif feeding girls.

—Black hair, complexion Latin, jewelled eyes
downcast . . . The slob beside her   feasts . . . What wonders is
she sitting on, over there?   15
The restaurant buzzes. She might as well be on Mars.
Where did it all go wrong? There ought to be a law against Henry.
—Mr. Bones: there is.

        —1964

Gwendolyn Brooks
1917–2000

WE REAL COOL

The Pool Players.
Seven at the Golden Shovel.

We real cool. We
Left school. We

Lurk late. We
Strike straight. We

Sing sin. We   5
Thin gin. We

Jazz June. We
Die soon.

—1960

Robert Lowell
1917–1977

FOR THE UNION DEAD

"Relinquunt Omnia Servare Rem Publicam."°

The old South Boston Aquarium stands
in a Sahara of snow now. Its broken windows are boarded.
The bronze weathervane cod has lost half its scales.
The airy tanks are dry.

"Relinquunt . . . Publicam" "They Gave up Everything to Preserve the Republic"

Once my nose crawled like a snail on the glass;   5
my hand tingled
to burst the bubbles
drifting from the noses of the cowed, compliant fish.

My hand draws back. I often sigh still
for the dark downward and vegetating kingdom   10
of the fish and reptile. One morning last March,
I pressed against the new barbed and galvanized

fence on the Boston Common. Behind their cage,
yellow dinosaur steamshovels were grunting
as they cropped up tons of mush and grass   15
to gouge their underworld garage.

Parking spaces luxuriate like civic
sandpiles in the heart of Boston.
A girdle of orange, Puritan-pumpkin colored girders
braces the tingling Statehouse,   20

shaking over the excavations, as it faces Colonel Shaw°
and his bell-cheeked Negro infantry
on St. Gaudens'° shaking Civil War relief,
propped by a plank splint against the garage's earthquake.

Two months after marching through Boston,   25
half the regiment was dead;
at the dedication,
William James° could almost hear the bronze Negroes breathe.

Their monument sticks like a fishbone
in the city's throat.   30
Its Colonel is as lean
as a compass-needle.

He has an angry wrenlike vigilance,
a greyhound's gentle tautness;
he seems to wince at pleasure,   35
and suffocate for privacy.

He is out of bounds now. He rejoices in man's lovely,
peculiar power to choose life and die—

---

21 Colonel Shaw Robert Gould Shaw (1837–1863) was commander of the first all-black regiment in the Union Army.   **23 St. Gaudens** American sculptor (1848–1907)
28 William James American philosopher (1842–1910)

when he leads his black soldiers to death,
he cannot bend his back.   40

On a thousand small town New England greens,
the old white churches hold their air
of sparse, sincere rebellion; frayed flags
quilt the graveyards of the Grand Army of the Republic.

The stone statues of the abstract Union Soldier   45
grow slimmer and younger each year—
wasp-waisted, they doze over muskets
and muse through their sideburns . . .

Shaw's father wanted no monument
except the ditch,   50
where his son's body was thrown
and lost with his "niggers."

The ditch is nearer.
There are no statues for the last war here;
on Boylston Street, a commercial photograph   55
shows Hiroshima boiling

over a Mosler Safe, the "Rock of Ages"
that survived the blast. Space is nearer.
When I crouch to my television set,
the drained faces of Negro school-children rise like balloons.   60

Colonel Shaw
is riding on his bubble,
he waits
for the blessèd break.

The Aquarium is gone. Everywhere,   65
giant finned cars nose forward like fish;
a savage servility
slides by on grease.

  —1959

Richard Wilbur
1 9 2 1 –

LOVE CALLS US TO
THE THINGS OF THIS WORLD

The eyes open to a cry of pulleys,
And spirited from sleep, the astounded soul
Hangs for a moment bodiless and simple
As false dawn.
              Outside the open window   5
The morning air is all awash with angels.
    Some are in bed-sheets, some are in blouses,
Some are in smocks: but truly there they are.
Now they are rising together in calm swells
Of halcyon feeling, filling whatever they wear   10
With the deep joy of their impersonal breathing;
    Now they are flying in place, conveying
The terrible speed of their omnipresence, moving
And staying like white water; and now of a sudden
They swoon down into so rapt a quiet   15
That nobody seems to be there.
                  The soul shrinks

    From all that it is about to remember,
From the punctual rape of every blessèd day,
And cries,   20
        "Oh, let there be nothing on earth but laundry,
Nothing but rosy hands in the rising steam
And clear dances done in the sight of heaven."
    Yet, as the sun acknowledges
With a warm look the world's hunks and colors,   25
The soul descends once more in bitter love
To accept the waking body, saying now
In a changed voice as the man yawns and rises,

    "Bring them down from their ruddy gallows;
Let there be clean linen for the backs of thieves;   30
Let lovers go fresh and sweet to be undone,
And the heaviest nuns walk in a pure floating
Of dark habits,
           keeping their difficult balance."

—1956

Philip Larkin
1 9 2 2 – 1 9 8 5

AUBADE

I work all day, and get half drunk at night.
Waking at four to soundless dark, I stare.
In time the curtain-edges will grow light.
Till then I see what's really always there:
Unresting death, a whole day nearer now,   5
Making all thought impossible but how
And where and when I shall myself die.
Arid interrogation: yet the dread
Of dying, and being dead,
Flashes afresh to hold and horrify.   10

The mind blanks at the glare. Not in remorse
—The good not done, the love not given, time
Torn off unused—nor wretchedly because
An only life can take so long to climb
Clear of its wrong beginnings, and may never;   15
But at the total emptiness for ever,
The sure extinction that we travel to
And shall be lost in always. Not to be here,
Not to be anywhere,
And soon; nothing more terrible, nothing more true.   20

This is a special way of being afraid
No trick dispels. Religion used to try,
That vast moth-eaten musical brocade
Created to pretend we never die,
And specious stuff that says *No rational being*   25
Can fear a thing it will not feel, not seeing
That this is what we fear—no sight, no sound,
No touch or taste or smell, nothing to think with,
Nothing to love or link with,
The anaesthetic from which none come round.   30

And so it stays just on the edge of vision,
A small unfocused blur, a standing chill
That slows each impulse down to indecision.
Most things may never happen: this one will,
And realization of it rages out   35
In furnace-fear when we are caught without

People or drink. Courage is no good:
It means not scaring others. Being brave
Lets no one off the grave.
Death is no different whined at than withstood.   40

Slowly light strengthens, and the room takes shape.
It stands plain as a wardrobe, what we know,
Have always known, know that we can't escape,
Yet can't accept. One side will have to go.
Meanwhile telephones crouch, getting ready to ring   45
In locked-up offices, and all the uncaring
Intricate rented world begins to rouse.
The sky is white as clay, with no sun.
Work has to be done.
Postmen like doctors go from house to house.   50

—1977

Allen Ginsberg
1926–1997

A SUPERMARKET IN CALIFORNIA

What thoughts I have of you tonight, Walt Whitman, for I
   walked down the sidestreets under the trees with a headache
   self-conscious looking at the full moon.
In my hungry fatigue, and shopping for images, I went into
   the neon fruit supermarket, dreaming of your enumerations!
What peaches and what penumbras! Whole families shopping at
   night! Aisles full of husbands! Wives in the avocados, babies
   in the tomatoes!—and you, Garcia Lorca,° what were you
   doing down by the watermelons?

I saw you, Walt Whitman, childless, lonely old grubber,
   poking among the meats in the refrigerator and eyeing the
   grocery boys.

---

3 **Garcia Lorca** Federico García Lorca, Spanish poet and dramatist (1899–1936)

I heard you asking questions of each: Who killed the pork chops?   5
  What price bananas? Are you my Angel?
I wandered in and out of the brilliant stacks of cans following you,
  and followed in my imagination by the store detective.
We strode down the open corridors together in our solitary fancy
  tasting artichokes, possessing every frozen delicacy, and never
  passing the cashier.

Where are we going, Walt Whitman? The doors close in an
  hour. Which way does your beard point tonight?
(I touch your book and dream of our odyssey in the supermarket and feel absurd.)
Will we walk all night through solitary streets? The trees add   10
  shade to shade, lights out in the houses, we'll both be lonely.
Will we stroll dreaming of the lost America of love past blue
  automobiles in driveways, home to our silent cottage?
Ah, dear father, graybeard, lonely old courage-teacher, what
  America did you have when Charon° quit poling his ferry
  and you got out on a smoking bank and stood watching the
  boat disappear on the black waters of Lethe?°

  —1955

John Ashbery
1 9 2 7 –

PARADOXES AND OXYMORONS

The poem is concerned with language on a very plain level.
Look at it talking to you. You look out a window
Or pretend to fidget. You have it but you don't have it.
You miss it, it misses you. You miss each other.

The poem is sad because it wants to be yours, and cannot.   5
What's a plain level? It is that and other things,

---

12 **Charon** in classical mythology, the ferryman who carried the dead across the river
Styx   **Lethe** another underworld river whose waters caused forgetfulness

Bringing a system of them into play. Play?
Well, actually, yes, but I consider play to be

A deeper outside thing, a dreamed role-pattern,
As in the division of grace these long August days   10
Without proof. Open-ended. And before you know
It gets lost in the steam and chatter of typewriters.

It has been played once more. I think you exist only
To tease me into doing it, on your level, and then you aren't there
Or have adopted a different attitude. And the poem   15
Has set me softly down beside you. The poem is you.

    —1981

James Wright
1927–1980

A BLESSING

Just off the highway to Rochester, Minnesota,
Twilight bounds softly forth on the grass.
And the eyes of those two Indian ponies
Darken with kindness.
They have come gladly out of the willows   5
To welcome my friend and me.
We step over the barbed wire into the pasture
Where they have been grazing all day, alone.
They ripple tensely, they can hardly contain their happiness
That we have come.   10
They bow shyly as wet swans. They love each other.
There is no loneliness like theirs.
At home once more,
They begin munching the young tufts of spring in the darkness.
I would like to hold the slenderer one in my arms,   15
For she has walked over to me
And nuzzled my left hand.
She is black and white,
Her mane falls wild on her forehead,
And the light breeze moves me to caress her long ear   20

That is delicate as the skin over a girl's wrist.
Suddenly I realize
That if I stepped out of my body I would break
Into blossom.

    —1961

Anne Sexton
1928–1974

CINDERELLA

You always read about it:
the plumber with twelve children
who wins the Irish Sweepstakes.
From toilets to riches.
That story.   5

Or the nursemaid,
some luscious sweet from Denmark
who captures the oldest son's heart.
From diapers to Dior.
That story.   10

Or a milkman who serves the wealthy,
eggs, cream, butter, yogurt, milk,
the white truck like an ambulance
who goes into real estate
and makes a pile.   15
From homogenized to martinis at lunch.

Or the charwoman
who is on the bus when it cracks up
and collects enough from the insurance.
From mops to Bonwit Teller.   20
That story.

Once
the wife of a rich man was on her deathbed

and she said to her daughter Cinderella:
Be devout. Be good. Then I will smile   25
down from heaven in the seam of a cloud.
The man took another wife who had
two daughters, pretty enough
but with hearts like blackjacks.
Cinderella was their maid.   30
She slept on the sooty hearth each night
and walked around looking like Al Jolson.
Her father brought presents home from town,
jewels and gowns for the other women
but the twig of a tree for Cinderella.   35
She planted that twig on her mother's grave
and it grew to a tree where a white dove sat.
Whenever she wished for anything the dove
would drop it like an egg upon the ground.
The bird is important, my dears, so heed him.   40

Next came the ball, as you all know.
It was a marriage market.
The prince was looking for a wife.
All but Cinderella were preparing
and gussying up for the big event.   45
Cinderella begged to go too.
Her stepmother threw a dish of lentils
into the cinders and said: Pick them
up in an hour and you shall go.
The white dove brought all his friends;   50
all the warm wings of the fatherland came,
and picked up the lentils in a jiffy.
No, Cinderella, said the stepmother,
you have no clothes and cannot dance.
That's the way with stepmothers.   55

Cinderella went to the tree at the grave
and cried forth like a gospel singer:
Mama! Mama! My turtledove,
send me to the prince's ball!
The bird dropped down a golden dress   60
and delicate little gold slippers.
Rather a large package for a simple bird.
So she went. Which is no surprise.
Her stepmother and sisters didn't
recognize her without her cinder face   65
and the prince took her hand on the spot
and danced with no other the whole day.

As nightfall came she thought she'd
better get home. The prince walked her home
and she disappeared into the pigeon house   70
and although the prince took an axe and broke
it open she was gone. Back to her cinders.
These events repeated themselves for three days.
However on the third day the prince
covered the palace steps with cobbler's wax   75
And Cinderella's gold shoe stuck upon it.

Now he would find whom the shoe fit
and find his strange dancing girl for keeps.
He went to their house and the two sisters
were delighted because they had lovely feet.   80
The eldest went into a room to try the slipper on
but her big toe got in the way so she simply
sliced it off and put on the slipper.
The prince rode away with her until the white dove
told him to look at the blood pouring forth.   85
That is the way with amputations.
They don't just heal up like a wish.
The other sister cut off her heel
but the blood told as blood will.
The prince was getting tired.   90
He began to feel like a shoe salesman.
But he gave it one last try.
This time Cinderella fit into the shoe
like a love letter into its envelope.

At the wedding ceremony   95
the two sisters came to curry favor
and the white dove pecked their eyes out.
Two hollow spots were left
like soup spoons.

Cinderella and the prince   100
lived, they say, happily ever after,
like two dolls in a museum case
never bothered by diapers or dust,
never arguing over the timing of an egg,
never telling the same story twice,   105
never getting a middle-aged spread,
their darling smiles pasted on for eternity
Regular Bobbsey Twins.
That story.

            —1970

Gary Snyder
1 9 3 0 –

A WALK

Sunday the only day we don't work:
Mules farting around the meadow,
     Murphy fishing,
The tent flaps in the warm
Early sun: I've eaten breakfast and I'll   5
       take a walk
To Benson Lake. Packed a lunch,
Goodbye. Hopping on creekbed boulders
Up the rock throat three miles
       Piute Creek—   10
In steep gorge glacier-slick rattlesnake country
Jump, land by a pool, trout skitter,
The clear sky. Deer tracks.
Bad place by a falls, boulders big as houses,
Lunch tied to belt,   15
I stemmed up a crack and almost fell
But rolled out safe on a ledge
      and ambled on.
Quail chicks freeze underfoot, color of stone
Then run cheep! away, hen quail fussing.   20
Craggy west end of Benson Lake—after edging
Past dark creek pools on a long white slope—
Lookt down in the ice-black lake
     lined with cliff
From far above: deep shimmering trout.   25
A lone duck in a gunsightpass
      steep side hill
Through slide-aspen and talus, to the east end
Down to grass, wading a wide smooth stream
Into camp. At last.   30
   By the rusty three-year-
Ago left-behind cookstove
Of the old trail crew,
Stoppt and swam and ate my lunch.
   —1968

Linda Pastan
1 9 3 2 –

ETHICS

In ethics class so many years ago
our teacher asked this question every fall:
if there were a fire in a museum
which would you save, a Rembrandt painting
or an old woman who hadn't many   5
years left anyhow? Restless on hard chairs
caring little for pictures or old age
we'd opt one year for life, the next for art
and always half-heartedly. Sometimes
the woman borrowed my grandmother's face   10
leaving her usual kitchen to wander
some drafty, half imagined museum.
One year, feeling clever, I replied
why not let the woman decide herself?
Linda, the teacher would report, eschews   15
the burdens of responsibility.
This fall in a real museum I stand
before a real Rembrandt, old woman,
or nearly so, myself. The colors
within this frame are darker than autumn,   20
darker even than winter—the browns of earth,
though earth's most radiant elements burn
through the canvas. I know now that woman
and painting and season are almost one
and all beyond saving by children.   25

—1980

Sylvia Plath
1932–1963

METAPHORS

I'm a riddle in nine syllables,
An elephant, a ponderous house,
A melon strolling on two tendrils.
O red fruit, ivory, fine timbers!
This loaf's big with its yeasty rising.   5
Money's new-minted in this fat purse.
I'm a means, a stage, a cow in calf.
I've eaten a bag of green apples,
Boarded the train there's no getting off.

—1960

DADDY

You do not do, you do not do
Any more, black shoe
In which I have lived like a foot
For thirty years, poor and white,
Barely daring to breathe or Achoo.   5

Daddy, I have had to kill you.
You died before I had time—
Marble-heavy, a bag full of God,
Ghastly statue with one gray toe
Big as a Frisco seal   10

And a head in the freakish Atlantic
Where it pours bean green over blue
In the waters off beautiful Nauset.
I used to pray to recover you.
Ach, du.   15

In the German tongue, in the Polish town
Scraped flat by the roller
Of wars, wars, wars.
But the name of the town is common.
My Polack friend   20

Says there are a dozen or two.
So I never could tell where you
Put your foot, your root,
I never could talk to you.
The tongue stuck in my jaw.   25

It stuck in a barb wire snare.
Ich, ich, ich, ich,
I could hardly speak.
I thought every German was you.
And the language obscene   30

An engine, an engine
Chuffing me off like a Jew.
A Jew to Dachau, Auschwitz, Belsen.
I began to talk like a Jew.
I think I may well be a Jew.   35

The snows of the Tyrol, the clear beer of Vienna
Are not very pure or true.
With my gypsy ancestress and my weird luck
And my Taroc pack and my Taroc pack
I may be a bit of a Jew.   40

I have always been scared of *you*,
With your Luftwaffe, your gobbledygoo.
And your neat mustache
And your Aryan eye, bright blue.
Panzer-man, panzer-man, O You—   45

Not God but a swastika
So black no sky could squeak through.
Every woman adores a Fascist,
The boot in the face, the brute
Brute heart of a brute like you.   50

You stand at the blackboard, daddy,
In the picture I have of you,
A cleft in your chin instead of your foot
But no less a devil for that, no not
Any less the black man who   55

Bit my pretty red heart in two.
I was ten when they buried you.
At twenty I tried to die
And get back, back, back to you.
I thought even the bones would do.   60

But they pulled me out of the sack,
And they stuck me together with glue.
And then I knew what to do.
I made a model of you,
A man in black with a Meinkampf° look   65

And a love of the rack and the screw.
And I said I do, I do.
So daddy, I'm finally through.
The black telephone's off at the root,
The voices just can't worm through.   70

If I've killed one man, I've killed two—
The vampire who said he was you
And drank my blood for a year,
Seven years, if you want to know.
Daddy, you can lie back now.   75

There's a stake in your fat black heart
And the villagers never liked you.
They are dancing and stamping on you.
They always *knew* it was you.
Daddy, daddy, you bastard, I'm through.   80

        —1965

Mark Strand
1 9 3 4 –

THE TUNNEL

A man has been standing
in front of my house
for days. I peek at him
from the living room
window and at night,   5

---

65 **Meinkampf**   *Mein Kampf* (My Battle) is Adolf Hitler's autobiography.

unable to sleep,
I shine my flashlight
down on the lawn.
He is always there.

After a while   10
I open the front door
just a crack and order
him out of my yard.
He narrows his eyes
and moans. I slam   15
the door and dash back
to the kitchen, then up
to the bedroom, then down.

I weep like a schoolgirl
and make obscene gestures   20
through the window. I
write large suicide notes
and place them so he
can read them easily.
I destroy the living   25
room furniture to prove
I own nothing of value.

When he seems unmoved
I decide to dig a tunnel
to a neighboring yard.   30
I seal the basement off
from the upstairs with
a brick wall. I dig hard
and in no time the tunnel
is done. Leaving my pick   35
and shovel below,

I come out in front of a house
and stand there too tired to
move or even speak, hoping
someone will help me.   40
I feel I'm being watched
and sometimes I hear
a man's voice,
but nothing is done
and I have been waiting for days.   45

    —1968

Mary Oliver
1 9 3 5 –

THE STORM

Now through the white orchard my little dog
    romps, breaking the new snow
    with wild feet.
Running here running there, excited,
    hardly able to stop, he leaps, he spins   5
until the white snow is written upon
    in large, exuberant letters,
a long sentence, expressing
    the pleasures of the body in this world.

Oh, I could not have said it better   10
    myself.
    —1999

Lucille Clifton
1 9 3 6 –

HOMAGE TO MY HIPS

these hips are big hips.
they need space to
move around in.
they don't fit into little
petty places. these hips   5
are free hips.
they don't like to be held back.
these hips have never been enslaved,
they go where they want to go
they do what they want to do.   10

these hips are mighty hips.
these hips are magic hips.
i have known them
to put a spell on a man and
spin him like a top!   15

   —1991

Marge Piercy
1936 –

BARBIE DOLL

This girlchild was born as usual
and presented dolls that did pee-pee
and miniature GE stoves and irons
and wee lipsticks the color of cherry candy.
Then in the magic of puberty, a classmate said: 5
You have a great big nose and fat legs.

She was healthy, tested intelligent,
possessed strong arms and back,
abundant sexual drive and manual dexterity.
She went to and fro apologizing.   10
Everyone saw a fat nose on thick legs.

She was advised to play coy,
exhorted to come on hearty,
exercise, diet, smile and wheedle.
Her good nature wore out   15
like a fan belt.

So she cut off her nose and her legs
and offered them up.
In the casket displayed on satin she lay
with the undertaker's cosmetics painted on,   20
a turned-up putty nose,
dressed in a pink and white nightie.

Doesn't she look pretty? everyone said.
Consummation at last.
To every woman a happy ending.   25

    —1969

Margaret Atwood
1 9 3 9 –

SIREN SONG°

This is the one song everyone
would like to learn: the song
that is irresistible:

the song that forces men
to leap overboard in squadrons   5
even though they see the beached skulls

the song nobody knows
because anyone who has heard it
is dead, and the others can't remember.

Shall I tell you the secret   10
and if I do, will you get me
out of this bird suit?

I don't enjoy it here
squatting on this island
looking picturesque and mythical   15

with these two feathery maniacs,
I don't enjoy singing
this trio, fatal and valuable.

Siren Song In Greek mythology, sirens were half-woman, half-bird creatures who lured
mariners to their deaths by enchanting them with their song.

I will tell the secret to you,
to you, only to you.   20
Come closer. This song

is a cry for help: Help me!
Only you, only you can,
you are unique

at last. Alas   25
it is a boring song
but it works every time.

       —1974

Seamus Heaney
1939 –

DIGGING

Between my finger and my thumb
The squat pen rests; snug as a gun.

Under my window, a clean rasping sound
When the spade sinks into gravelly ground:
My father, digging. I look down   5

Till his straining rump among the flowerbeds
Bends low, comes up twenty years away
Stooping in rhythm through potato drills
Where he was digging.

The coarse boot nestled on the lug, the shaft   10
Against the inside knee was levered firmly.
He rooted out tall tops, buried the bright edge deep
To scatter new potatoes that we picked
Loving their cool hardness in our hands.

By God, the old man could handle a spade.   15
Just like his old man.

My grandfather cut more turf in a day
Than any other man on Toner's bog.
Once I carried him milk in a bottle
Corked sloppily with paper. He straightened up   20
To drink it, then fell to right away

Nicking and slicing neatly, heaving sods
Over his shoulder, going down and down
For the good turf. Digging.

The cold smell of potato mould, the squelch and slap   25
Of soggy peat, the curt cuts of an edge
Through living roots awaken in my head.
But I've no spade to follow men like them.

Between my finger and my thumb
The squat pen rests.   30
I'll dig with it.

    —1966

Sharon Olds
1 9 4 2 –

THE ONE GIRL
AT THE BOYS' PARTY

When I take my girl to the swimming party
I set her down among the boys. They tower and
bristle, she stands there smooth and sleek,
her math scores unfolding in the air around her.
They will strip to their suits, her body hard and   5
indivisible as a prime number,
they'll plunge into the deep end, she'll subtract
her height from ten feet, divide it into
hundreds of gallons of water, the numbers
bouncing in her mind like molecules of chlorine   10

in the bright blue pool. When they climb out,
her ponytail will hang its pencil lead
down her back, her narrow silk suit
with hamburgers and french fries printed on it
will glisten in the brilliant air, and they will   15
see her sweet face, solemn and
sealed, a factor of one, and she will
see their eyes, two each,
their legs, two each, and the curves of their sexes,
one each, and in her head she'll be doing her   20
wild multiplying, as the drops
sparkle and fall to the power of a thousand from her body.

   —1983

Louise Glück
1 9 4 3 –

THE SCHOOL CHILDREN

The children go forward with their little satchels.
And all morning the mothers have labored
to gather the late apples, red and gold,
like words of another language.

And on the other shore   5
are those who wait behind great desks
to receive these offerings.

How orderly they are—the nails
on which the children hang
their overcoats of blue or yellow wool.   10

And the teachers shall instruct them in silence
and the mothers shall scour the orchards for a way out,
drawing to themselves the gray limbs of the fruit trees
bearing so little ammunition.

   —1971

Yusef Komunyakaa
1 9 4 7 –

FACING IT

My black face fades,
hiding inside the black granite.
I said I wouldn't,
dammit: No tears.
I'm stone. I'm flesh.   5
My clouded reflection eyes me
like a bird of prey, the profile of night
slanted against morning. I turn
this way—the stone lets me go.
I turn that way—I'm inside   10
the Vietnam Veterans Memorial
again, depending on the light
to make a difference.
I go down the 58,022 names,
half-expecting to find   15
my own in letters like smoke.
I touch the name Andrew Johnson;
I see the booby trap's white flash.
Names shimmer on a woman's blouse
but when she walks away   20
the names stay on the wall.
Brushstrokes flash, a red bird's
wings cutting across my stare.
The sky. A plane in the sky.
A white vet's image floats   25
closer to me, then his pale eyes
look through mine. I'm a window.
He's lost his right arm
inside the stone. In the black mirror
a woman's trying to erase names: 30
No, she's brushing a boy's hair.

—1988

Leslie Marmon Silko
1948 –

PRAYER TO THE PACIFIC

I traveled to the ocean
        distant
             from my southwest land of sandrock
             to the moving blue water.
        Big as the myth of origin.   5

Pale
pale water in the yellow-white light of
             sun   floating west
               to China
             where ocean herself was born.   10
Clouds that blow across the sand are wet.

Squat in the wet sand and speak to the Ocean:
        I return to you   turquoise   the red coral you sent us,
             sister spirit of Earth.
Four round stones in my pocket. I carry back the ocean   15
             to suck and to taste.

Thirty thousand years ago
             Indians came riding across the ocean
             carried by giant sea turtles.

Waves were high that day   20
        great sea turtles waded   slowly out
             from the gray sundown sea.

Grandfather Turtle rolled in the sand   four times
          and disappeared
             swimming into the sun.   25

And so   from that time
      immemorial,
             as the old people say,
rain clouds drift from the west
             gift from the ocean.   30

Green leaves in the wind
Wet earth on my feet
     swallowing raindrops
            clear from China.

—1981

Timothy Steele
1 9 4 8 –

AN AUBADE

As she is showering, I wake to see
A shine of earrings on the bedside stand,
A single yellow sheet which, over me,
Has folds as intricate as drapery
In paintings from some fine old master's hand.   5

The pillow which, in dozing, I embraced
Retains the salty sweetness of her skin;
I sense her smooth back, buttocks, belly, waist,
The leggy warmth which spread and gently laced
Around my legs and loins, and drew me in.   10

I stretch and curl about a bit and hear her
Singing among the water's hiss and race.
Gradually the early light makes clearer
The perfume bottles by the dresser's mirror,
The silver flashlight, standing on its face,   15

Which shares the corner of the dresser with
An ivy spilling tendrils from a cup.
And so content am I, I can forgive
Pleasure for being brief and fugitive.
I'll stretch some more, but postpone getting up   20

Until she finishes her shower and dries
(Now this and now that foot placed on a chair)

Her fineboned ankles, and her calves and thighs,
The pink full nipples of her breasts, and ties
Her towel up, turban-style, about her hair.   25

—1986

Carolyn Forché
1 9 5 0 –

THE COLONEL

What you have heard is true. I was in his house. His wife carried a
tray of coffee and sugar. His daughter filed her nails, his son went
out for the night. There were daily papers, pet dogs, a pistol on the
cushion beside him. The moon swung bare on its black cord over
the house. On the television was a cop show. It was in English. Bro-   5
ken bottles were embedded in the walls around the house to scoop
the kneecaps from a man's legs or cut his hands to lace. On the windows there were gratings like those in liquor stores. We had dinner,
rack of lamb, good wine, a gold bell was on the table for calling the
maid. The maid brought green mangoes, salt, a type of bread. I was   10
asked how I enjoyed the country. There was a brief commercial in
Spanish. His wife took everything away. There was some talk then
of how difficult it had become to govern. The parrot said hello on
the terrace. The colonel told it to shutup, and pushed himself from
the table. My friend said to me with his eyes: say nothing. The   15
colonel returned with a sack used to bring groceries home. He
spilled many human ears on the table. They were like dried peach
halves. There is no other way to say this. He took one of them in
his hands, shook it in our faces, dropped it into a water glass. It
came alive there. I am tired of fooling around he said. As for the   20
rights of anyone, tell your people they can go fuck themselves. He
swept the ears to the floor with his arm and held the last of his wine
in the air. Something for your poetry, no? he said. Some of the ears
on the floor caught this scrap of his voice. Some of the ears on the
floor were pressed to the ground.   25

—1978

Joy Harjo
1951 –

EAGLE POEM

To pray you open your whole self
To sky, to earth, to sun, to moon
To one whole voice that is you.
And know there is more
That you can't see, can't hear,   5
Can't know except in moments
Steadily growing, and in languages
That aren't always sound but other
Circles of motion.

     —1990

Rita Dove
1952 –

DAYSTAR

She wanted a little room for thinking:
but she saw diapers steaming on the line,
a doll slumped behind the door.
So she lugged a chair behind the garage
to sit out the children's naps.   5

Sometimes there were things to watch—
the pinched armor of a vanished cricket,
a floating maple leaf. Other days
she stared until she was assured
when she closed her eyes   10
she'd see only her own vivid blood.

She had an hour, at best, before Liza appeared
pouting from the top of the stairs.
And just *what* was mother doing
out back with the field mice? Why,   15

building a palace. Later
that night when Thomas rolled over and
lurched into her, she would open her eyes
and think of the place that was hers
for an hour—where   20
she was nothing,
pure nothing, in the middle of the day.

    —1986

Naomi Shihab Nye
1952 –

THE TRAVELING ONION

*"It is believed that the onion originally came from India. In Egypt
it was an object of worship—why, I haven't been able to find out.
From Egypt the onion entered Greece and on to Italy, thence into
all of Europe."*   —Better Living Cookbook

When I think how far the onion has traveled
just to enter my stew today, I could kneel and praise
all small forgotten miracles,
crackly paper peeling on the drainboard,
pearly layers in smooth agreement,   5
the way knife enters onion
and onion falls apart on the chopping block,
a history revealed.

And I would never scold the onion
for causing tears.   10
It is right that tears fall

for something small and forgotten.
How at meal, we sit to eat,
commenting on texture of meat or herbal aroma
but never on the translucence of onion,   15
now limp, now divided,
or its traditionally honorable career:
For the sake of others,
disappear.

  —1986

Gary Soto
1 9 5 2 –

ORANGES

The first time I walked
With a girl, I was twelve,
Cold, and weighted down
With two oranges in my jacket.
December. Frost cracking   5
Beneath my steps, my breath
Before me, then gone,
As I walked toward
Her house, the one whose
Porch light burned yellow   10
Night and day, in any weather.
A dog barked at me, until
She came out pulling
At her gloves, face bright
With rouge. I smiled,   15
Touched her shoulder, and led
Her down the street, across
A used car lot and a line
Of newly planted trees,

Until we were breathing   20
Before a drugstore. We
Entered, the tiny bell
Bringing a saleslady
Down a narrow aisle of goods.
I turned to the candies   25
Tiered like bleachers,
And asked what she wanted—
Light in her eyes, a smile
Starting at the corners
Of her mouth. I fingered   30
A nickel in my pocket,
And when she lifted a chocolate
That cost a dime,
I didn't say anything.
I took the nickel from   35
My pocket, then an orange,
And set them quietly on
The counter. When I looked up,
The lady's eyes met mine,
And held them, knowing   40
Very well what it was all
About.
      Outside,
A few cars hissing past,
Fog hanging like old   45
Coats between the trees.
I took my girl's hand
In mine for two blocks,
Then released it to let
Her unwrap the chocolate.   50
I peeled my orange
That was so bright against
The gray of December
That, from some distance,
Someone might have thought   55
I was making a fire in my hands.

    —1995

Julia Alvarez
1 9 5 3 –

BILINGUAL SESTINA

Some things I have to say aren't getting said
in this snowy, blond, blue-eyed, gum-chewing English:
dawn's early light sifting through *persianas* closed
the night before by dark-skinned girls whose words
evoke *cama, aposento, sueños* in *nombres*   5
from that first world I can't translate from Spanish.

Gladys, Rosario, Altagracia—the sounds of Spanish
wash over me like warm island waters as I say
your soothing names: a child again learning the *nombres*
of things you point to in the world before English   10
turned *sol, sierra, cielo, luna* to vocabulary words—
sun, earth, sky, moon. Language closed

like the touch-sensitive *morivivi* whose leaves closed
when we kids poked them, astonished. Even Spanish
failed us back then when we saw how frail a word is   15
when faced with the thing it names. How saying
its name won't always summon up in Spanish or English
the full blown genie from the bottled *nombre.*

Gladys, I summon you back by saying your *nombre.*
Open up again the house of slatted windows closed   20
since childhood, where *palabras* left behind for English
stand dusty and awkward in neglected Spanish.
Rosario, muse of *el patio,* sing in me and through me say
that world again, begin first with those first words

you put in my mouth as you pointed to the world—   25
not Adam, not God, but a country girl numbering
the stars, the blades of grass, warming the sun by saying,
¡Qué calor! as you opened up the morning closed
inside the night until you sang in Spanish,
Estas son las mañanitas, and listening in bed, no English   30

yet in my head to confuse me with translations, no English
doubling the world with synonyms, no dizzying array of words
—the world was simple and intact in Spanish—

luna, sol, casa, luz, flor, as if the *nombres*
were the outer skin of things, as if words were so close   35
one left a mist of breath on things by saying

their names, an intimacy I now yearn for in English—
words so close to what I mean that I almost hear my Spanish
heart beating, beating inside what I say *en inglés.*

—1995

Mary Jo Salter
1 9 5 4 –

BOULEVARD DU MONTPARNASSE

Once, in a doorway in Paris, I saw
the most beautiful couple in the world.
They were each the single most beautiful thing in the world.
She would have been sixteen, perhaps; he twenty.
Their skin was the same shade of black: like a shiny Steinway.   5
And they stood there like the four-legged instrument
of a passion so grand one could barely imagine them
ever working, or eating, or reading a magazine.
Even they could hardly believe it.
Her hands gripped his belt loops, as they found each other's eyes,   10
because beauty like this must be held onto,
could easily run away on the power
of his long, lean thighs; or the tiny feet of her laughter.
I thought: now I will write a poem,
set in a doorway on the Boulevard du Montparnasse,   15
in which the brutishness of time
rates only a mention; I will say simply
that if either one should ever love another,
a greater beauty shall not be the cause.

—1994

Cathy Song
1 9 5 5 –

LOST SISTER

I

In China,
even the peasants
named their first daughters
Jade—
the stone that in the far fields   5
could moisten the dry season,
could make men move mountains
for the healing green of the inner hills
glistening like slices of winter melon.

And the daughters were grateful: 10
they never left home.
To move freely was a luxury
stolen from them at birth.
Instead, they gathered patience,
learning to walk in shoes   15
the size of teacups,
without breaking—
the arc of their movements
as dormant as the rooted willow,
as redundant as the farmyard hens.   20
But they traveled far
in surviving,
learning to stretch the family rice,
to quiet the demons,
the noisy stomachs.   25

2

There is a sister
across the ocean,
who relinquished her name,
diluting jade green
with the blue of the Pacific.   30
Rising with a tide of locusts,
she swarmed with others
to inundate another shore.
In America,
there are many roads   35
and women can stride along with men.

But in another wilderness,
the possibilities,
the loneliness,
can strangulate like jungle vines.   40
The meager provisions and sentiments
of once belonging—
fermented roots, Mah-Jongg tiles and firecrackers—
set but a flimsy household
in a forest of nightless cities.   45
A giant snake rattles above,
spewing black clouds into your kitchen.
Dough-faced landlords
slip in and out of your keyholes,
making claims you don't understand,   50
tapping into your communication systems
of laundry lines and restaurant chains.

You find you need China:
your one fragile identification,
a jade link   55
handcuffed to your wrist.
You remember your mother
who walked for centuries,
footless—
and like her,   60
you have left no footprints,
but only because
there is an ocean in between,
the unremitting space of your rebellion.

    —1983

Li-Young Lee
1 9 5 7 –

EATING TOGETHER

In the steamer is the trout
seasoned with slivers of ginger,
two sprigs of green onion, and sesame oil.
We shall eat it with rice for lunch,
brothers, sister, my mother who will   5
taste the sweetest meat of the head,
holding it between her fingers
deftly, the way my father did
weeks ago. Then he lay down
to sleep like a snow-covered road   10
winding through pines older than him,
without any travelers, and lonely for no one.

—1985

Rafael Campo
1 9 6 4 –

THE NEXT POEM
COULD BE YOUR LAST

Imagine death. No fun. No poetry.
No further arguments with relatives.
No work to do. No boring life to live.
Imagine, death: like making pottery
Or writing eulogies, it takes some skill   5
To do it passably. Like argument,
It needs resistance to be shaped against.
Like relatives you fight the urge to kill,
You know you won't. Like work, there's never less
Of it. Imagine: death is almost life.   10
Except it's fascinating, like a knife.
You lose yourself just staring at the edge.
You lose yourself and suddenly you're not
Alive, you're dying and for fun you try
To write your eulogy. You tell some lies,   15
Pretend you're wry and brave. Imagine that.

    —1996

Author
Biographies

Sir Walter Raleigh

To his contemporaries, Sir Walter Raleigh (ca. 1552–1618) represented the Elizabethan Renaissance ideal of the complete individual. Raleigh was a poet, historian, courtier, explorer, colonist, seaman, soldier, and diplomat. The fact that he more often than not failed at his many pursuits did not interfere with his symbolic stature. Found guilty of conspiring against the newly installed King James I, Raleigh was sentenced to death in 1603 and spent fifteen years imprisoned in the Tower of London before his execution in 1618. His poetry is informed with a keen awareness of the transitory nature of existence.

Michael Drayton

Like Shakespeare, Michael Drayton (1563–1631) was born in Warwickshire. He wrote many different kinds of poems: sonnets, odes, pastorals, poetic epistles, and verse histories. The sonnet in this text is from *Idea's Mirror*, a sonnet sequence Drayton first issued in 1594 but continued to revise and reissue until 1619. The sequence celebrates his devotion to Lady Rainsford (Anne Goodere), called "Idea" in the sonnets.

Christopher Marlowe

Christopher Marlowe (1564–1593) led a brief life filled with controversy. At Corpus Christi College, Cambridge, college authorities hesitated to grant him his degree, apparently dubious about his frequent absences and suspicious of his political loyalties. A letter from the Privy Council implied that his absences were spent in service to Queen Elizabeth, and the degree was granted. In 1589, he and fellow poet Thomas Watson were jailed on charges of murder for their part in a street fight in which a young man was killed, but both were later released. In May 1593, playwright Thomas Kyd testified before a government council that Marlowe was an atheist, a charge later repeated by a government informant; Marlowe was questioned and released. Twelve days later, in the company of notorious spy Robert Poley, Marlowe was killed in a tavern, supposedly over a dispute concerning the bill. Many have speculated that he was, rather, murdered for political reasons. After Shakespeare, Marlowe was the greatest dramatic writer in English during the sixteenth century. His masterpieces are *Tamburlaine* and *Doctor Faustus*, and his major poetic work is *Hero and Leander*, an original treatment of the mythical story of two drowned lovers. In "The Passionate Shepherd to His Love," one of his most famous lyrics, Marlowe adopts the conventions of pastoral poetry (a conventional mode that celebrates the innocent life of shepherds and shepherdesses).

William Shakespeare

Many consider William Shakespeare (1564–1616) to be the greatest English writer of all time. His achievement is so awe-inspiring that some scholars suggest his amazing output could not possibly be the work of one man (and that man an actor of modest educational background). Shakespeare was born the son of a merchant in Stratford-upon-Avon. In 1582, he married Anne Hathaway, with whom he had three children. While there are many gaps in his life story, we know that by 1592 he was a successful dramatist and actor in London. His tragedies, comedies, and histories have made him the world's most famous and most produced playwright. In the mid-1590s, Shakespeare wrote 154 sonnets, which were not published until 1609. Sonnets 1–126 are addressed to a handsome young man who is also a beloved friend. Sonnets 127–152 are addressed to the "Dark Lady," a dark-haired beauty with whom the speaker has a passionate but tempestuous relationship.

Thomas Campion

Thomas Campion (1567–1620) was a physician, music and literary theorist, composer, and poet. He coupled his lyric poems with music of his own composition to produce lasting works of art. An ardent admirer of John Donne and metaphysical poetry, Campion differs from the Metaphysicals by being concerned more with auditory effects than with the dramatic effects of images. He also departs from conventional Elizabethan poetic practice in preferring to describe music, movement, and change in the natural world, rather than using visual imagery to paint static portraits.

John Donne

John Donne (1572–1631) was born into a Roman Catholic family when anti-Catholic feeling in England was especially strong. He left the church in the 1590s and lived a restless and sometimes rakish life. Donne advanced to the position of private secretary to Sir Thomas Egerton, the Lord Keeper, but lost the post when he married the young niece of his employer in 1601. For the next dozen years, Donne struggled through several jobs, barely supporting his growing family. In 1615, he was ordained an Anglican priest and soon became one of the church's great preachers and sermon writers. From 1621 until his death he was Dean of St. Paul's Cathedral in London. His poetry is often divided into two periods: the secular, often bawdy love poems of his early years, and the religious poetry—some of the best written in English—of his later years. His poetry employs bold images and challenging conceits, and while his rhythms are frequently colloquial, they just as frequently contain complicated metrical patterns and abstruse grammar.

Ben Jonson

The first half of Ben Jonson's (1573?–1637) life was especially turbulent. After his father's early death, he was adopted by a bricklayer; in the army, he survived hand-to-hand combat; he killed a fellow actor in a duel in 1595, narrowly escaping the gallows; he converted to Catholicism at a time when anti-Catholic sentiment was strong; he was imprisoned for insulting Scotland just after King James arrived in London; in 1605, he was suspected in the Gunpowder Plot of Guy Fawkes against the Protestant government of King James. Yet he survived all of this to become a major literary figure of his time. He wrote plays (including *The Alchemist* and *Volpone*), masques (which were especially popular in the court of King James), criticism, and many types of poetry. He especially enjoyed the life of the tavern, where he would discuss literature and the work of writers seeking his advice. His influence was so strong that poets like Thomas Carew and Robert Herrick called themselves "sons of Ben."

Robert Herrick

The son of a goldsmith, Robert Herrick (1591–1674) was born in London and took his M.A. at Cambridge. While he might have preferred to spend his time in London with his mentor Ben Jonson, he was ordained to the ministry and sent to Dean Prior, a country parish in Devonshire. There he wrote most of his poetry, which features a polished style and light touch. Herrick lost his parish when the Puritans came to power, but he was returned to Dean Prior in 1662 after the restoration of the monarchy.

George Herbert

After taking his degrees at Cambridge, George Herbert (1593–1633) was elected Public Orator of the University; this office called on him to express the official university statement in Latin on public occasions. Although the position gave him prominence, he did not use his visibility to advance himself. He married in 1629 and entered the priesthood in 1630. He distinguished himself in his three short years as a priest by his extraordinary devotion to his parishioners. Although Herbert became a priest only three years before his death in 1633 from consumption, all of his extant poems are primarily devotional.

John Milton

John Milton (1608–1674) was born in London and educated at Cambridge University. He served as Oliver Cromwell's Latin secretary and wrote tracts defending the Puritan Parliament and its execution of Charles I. In 1652, he lost his eyesight from overexertion, a tragedy he addresses in "When I Consider How My Light Is Spent." Milton defended the Puritan government until its end, and for a brief period after the Restoration of Charles II in 1660, he was imprisoned and threatened with execution. Following his release, he dedicated himself to his poetry. His masterpiece, *Paradise Lost*, is one of English literature's supreme achievements. Published in 1667, the epic poem tells of God's creation of the universe, Satan's rebellion, and the Fall of Adam and Eve through original sin.

Anne Bradstreet

Anne Bradstreet (1612?–1672) immigrated to America in 1630; both her father and husband held major offices in the colony. In 1650, her brother-in-law, while on business in London, published Bradstreet's first collection of poetry without her knowledge. Her reaction to seeing the volume is the subject of "The Author to Her Book." A frontier woman who confronted hardships and tragedy, Bradstreet still managed to write some of the finest Puritan poetry extant. The directness and force of her domestic poetry give insight into the Puritan mind and lifestyle, while often diffusing stereotypical notions of Puritan life—as, for example, in "To My Dear and Loving Husband," where Bradstreet expresses her passion for her absent husband.

Richard Lovelace

Richard Lovelace (1618–1658) was one of the chief Cavalier poets, a group of writers who supported Charles I in the Civil War and composed elegant poems on the themes of love, war, chivalry, and loyalty to the King. Handsome, well educated, and witty, Lovelace was for a time the model courtier. During the Civil War, however, he was imprisoned and then exiled from England. While abroad, he hired himself out as a soldier of fortune and was severely wounded in battle. He returned to England, only to be imprisoned once again. Upon his release, he found himself impoverished and unemployed; he died shortly after.

Andrew Marvell

Andrew Marvell (1621–1678) was educated at Trinity College, Cambridge. He was sympathetic to the Crown until his appointment as tutor to Mary Fairfax, daughter of one of Cromwell's generals, at which time he switched his loyalty to the Puritan cause. Marvell later served under Cromwell as Assistant Latin Secretary, and he soon became a close friend of Milton. After Cromwell's death, Marvell entered Parliament, where he served for almost twenty years. During the Restoration, he wrote bitter satires in prose and verse that, while not read much today, brought him some fame in his time. Today, we remember him for his lyric poetry. "To His Coy Mistress" is an example of *carpe diem* lyric—poetry exhorting listeners to "seize the day, for tomorrow we die"—noteworthy especially for its wit and playful irony.

Jonathan Swift

Jonathan Swift (1667–1745), generally considered the greatest prose satirist in the English language, was born to poor English parents in Dublin. He was educated at Trinity College and went to England in 1689 to serve as undersecretary to statesman and writer Sir William Temple. Under Temple, Swift read widely, discovered his talent for satire, and met Esther Johnson, a lifelong intimate who was the "Stella" to whom Swift addressed the letters published as *Journal to Stella*. In 1694 Swift took orders as a priest in the Church of England, and in 1713 he became Dean of St. Patrick's in Dublin, an office he served diligently, with an abiding concern for Ireland's poor. Swift held this position until 1742, when a more or less complete physical collapse caused him to be placed under the care of guardians. He is best known today for *Gulliver's Travels* and "A Modest Proposal," two celebrated examples of political satire.

Alexander Pope

Born into a Roman Catholic family in a Protestant state, Alexander Pope (1688–1744) endured a life full of hardships. When he was twelve, his family was forced to move to Binfield in Windsor Forest to comply with a recently passed ordinance forbidding Catholics to live within ten miles of London. As a young man, Pope (like all professed Catholics) was barred from attending university. Poor health plagued Pope throughout his life, and his growth was stunted and deformed by curvature of the spine. Despite these difficulties, Pope became the most successful writer of his time and the first English writer to earn his living from writing. Especially profitable were his translations of *The Iliad* and *The Odyssey*. Although much of his original poetry is satirical (among his best satires are *The Rape of the Lock* and *The Dunciad*), he also wrote pastorals, epigrams, and philosophical poems, of which *An Essay on Man* is an important example.

Phillis Wheatley

Born in present-day Gambia, Phillis Wheatley (1753?–1784) was kidnapped and sold into slavery when she was roughly seven years old. She lived in Boston with her owners, John and Susanna Wheatley, who encouraged her to read and write. In 1773, she accompanied the Wheatleys to London, where a collection of her poems was published and celebrated. This collection is generally thought to have been the first book published by a black American. After gaining her freedom, she married John Peters, another free black. The couple struggled to support themselves and their three children (all of whom would die in childhood). At the age of thirty-one, Wheatley died in poverty and obscurity. Her poetry tends to be neo-classical in style and usually religious or topical in theme, frequently celebrating a hopeful vision of America. "To the University of Cambridge" reminds the students of Harvard not to forget their Christian roots.

William Blake

Born in London, William Blake (1757–1827) was self-educated and earned a meager living as an engraver. Most of his poetry can be divided into two categories: lyrical poems and longer, prophetic works. The lyrical poems include his *Songs of Innocence* (1789), which offer a non-threatening and hopeful vision of the world, and his *Songs of Experience* (1794), which present a bleaker and more ambivalent vision of reality. His lyrical poems tend to be lucid and accessible. In 1789 he issued *The Book of Thel*, the first of his prophetic books, all of which are daring, mystical, and labyrinthine. Blake created engravings to illustrate many of his poems, including "The Sick Rose." Judged on their own merit, the engravings stand as first-rate works of art. The poems in this volume are from Blake's *Songs of Experience*.

William Wordsworth

William Wordsworth (1770–1850) grew up in the Lake District of England and was educated at Cambridge University. While in France during the early stages of the Revolution, he fell in love with a young French woman with whom he had a daughter. Poverty pulled the lovers apart, and Wordsworth returned to England. By the time he could send for his family, the couple had drifted apart emotionally. In 1795, a friend left Wordsworth a legacy sufficient enough to allow him to live solely by his poetry. At this time, Wordsworth settled down with his sister Dorothy, who became his secretary and a major inspiration. By no later than 1797 Wordsworth had met Samuel Taylor Coleridge and, in 1798, the two poets issued the *Lyrical Ballads*, a volume that ushered in the Romantic era in English poetry. In 1802, Wordsworth married Mary Hutchinson, with whom he had five children. Although he had written his greatest poetry by 1807, fame and prosperity came slowly. In 1843 he was appointed Poet Laureate.

Samuel Taylor Coleridge

The son of a clergyman, Samuel Taylor Coleridge (1772–1834) left Cambridge University before receiving his degree. After leaving school, he and fellow poet Robert Southey devised plans for an ideal democratic community in America, but the scheme collapsed. Shortly thereafter, Coleridge met William Wordsworth, beginning an intense if turbulent personal and creative relationship that spanned the remainder of his life. Coleridge is perhaps remembered chiefly for his collaboration with Wordsworth on *Lyrical*

Ballads (1798), which heralded the English Romantic era, and his *Biographia Literaria* (1817), widely considered the most important work of general literary criticism produced in the era. His poetry, though not large in quantity, is frequently extraordinary. Coleridge was attracted to the idea of a "universal life consciousness," which he explored in part through experimentation with opiates and attempted to articulate in his poetry. When his exploration of these ideas was at its most intense, he wrote "Kubla Khan" under the influence of laudanum. Frequently challenged by poor health, Coleridge began taking large doses of opium for attacks of rheumatism. Gradually becoming addicted to the drug, he separated from his wife, Sara Fricker, and, increasingly depressed, was more and more frequently beset by terrifying nightmares. His life took a turn for the better when he rediscovered consolation in Christianity and, specifically, the Anglican Church in the second decade of the nineteenth century. Coleridge died in 1834 a respected member of the literary community.

George Gordon, Lord Byron

The details of Byron's (1788–1824) life have long threatened to obscure his output as a writer. At Cambridge, he piled up debts and became known as an atheist and a radical. To compensate for his club foot, which required painful medical treatment, Byron concentrated on developing his athletic ability, particularly as a swimmer. His outspoken views, good looks, and athleticism (along with a pet bear that was his constant companion) contributed to his high social visibility. At nineteen, he published *Hours of Idleness*, his first collection of lyric poetry. Beginning in 1809, he traveled throughout Europe, where he cultivated his reputation as a poet. Known for his obsessive, unscrupulous womanizing—his lover Lady Caroline Lamb famously characterized him as "mad, bad and dangerous to know"—Byron seems to have begun an intimate relationship with his half-sister Augusta in 1813. Byron married Anne Milbanke early in 1815, but the union lasted only a year. After his good friend and fellow poet Percy Shelley died in 1822, Byron moved from Pisa to Genoa and, in 1823, sailed to Greece to aid that country in its struggle with the Turks. He died on the battlefield in 1824 from malaria. As a poet, Byron is best known for several lyric poems (two of which are included in this text) and the long poems *Childe Harold's Pilgrimage* (1812–1818) and *Don Juan* (1819–1824).

Percy Bysshe Shelley

Percy Bysshe Shelley's (1792–1822) life and work throve on controversy. Raised in a conservative household with a father who served in Parliament, Shelley was expelled from Oxford for co-authoring a pamphlet on atheism. Shelley, whose slight build brought him ridicule as a child, fought from his college days on against all forms of tyranny. Although he married at age eighteen, he saw marriage as an oppressive and degrading social system. In 1813, as a disciple of the radical social philosopher William Godwin, Shelley wrote his first major work, *Queen Mab*. Mab predicts the downfall of social institutions and a return to a more natural state of happiness. In 1814, Shelley fell in love with Godwin's daughter Mary Wollstonecraft and abandoned his first wife. He and Mary fled to France, where he invited his first wife to live with them as a sister. Two years later, his first wife drowned herself, and Shelley was denied custody of their two children; he was stigmatized as an atheist, revolutionary, and complete degenerate. Shelley subsequently married Mary and moved to Italy. He drowned when his boat was caught in a sudden squall on the Gulf of Spezzia. His major works include *Prometheus Unbound*, *Adonais*, and "Ode to the West Wind."

John Keats

John Keats (1795–1821) left school at age fifteen and was apprenticed to a surgeon and apothecary; he received his license in 1816. Soon after, however, he abandoned medicine and turned to poetry. The speed of his poetic development was amazing. In 1816, he wrote one of English literature's major sonnets, "On First Looking into Chapman's Homer," and in 1817, he wrote *Endymion*, a 4,000-line allegory about a poet's search for ideal beauty and happiness. In 1818, he nursed his brother Tom, who, like their mother and the poet himself, died of tuberculosis. After his brother's death, Keats became engaged to Fanny Brawne, but his poverty, increasingly poor health, and obsession with poetry made marriage an impossibility. In 1819, Keats produced major work after major work, including "The Eve of St. Agnes," "La Belle Dame sans Merci," *Lamia*, and all six of his great odes.

Elizabeth Barrett Browning

Elizabeth Barrett (1806–1861) was born into a strict household, where illness and then-current notions of the care of invalids (especially female invalids) confined her. One of the era's favorite legends is how a passionate Robert Browning rescued her from her home by elopement in 1846. Although she was at the time forty years old and a well-established poet, her father bitterly opposed the marriage and was never reconciled to his daughter. The couple settled in Italy, where Barrett Browning became a strong voice for Italian independence and spoke out forcefully against slavery in the United States. Her most famous work is her *Sonnets from the Portuguese* (1850), a sequence of forty-four sonnets which records the stages of her love for her husband and includes "How Do I Love Thee?".

Edgar Allan Poe

Before Edgar Allan Poe (1809–1849) was three, his father deserted him and his mother died. He was subsequently taken in by the Allan family of Richmond, Virginia. In 1826, Poe attended the University of Virginia, but he was forced to leave when his foster father refused to cover his gambling debts. In 1827, he published his first volume of poems, *Tamerlane and Other Poems*. He then enlisted in the army and later enrolled at West Point, from which he was dishonorably discharged. (Poe, who was unhappy as a cadet, seems to have connived at his own discharge.) Poe constantly battled poverty, anxiety, and tragedy, suffering through the deaths of his mother, foster mother, and wife. He was dismissed from several editorial posts because of his personal instability. Yet during his short life, Poe created a remarkable body of work. He was a brilliant editor; an innovative critical theorist; a short story writer who contributed to the development of the modern short story, detective fiction, and science fiction; and the author of forty-eight influential and symbolic poems. "The Raven," reprinted in this anthology, brought him considerable fame (but little income) during his lifetime.

Alfred, Lord Tennyson

Alfred Tennyson (1809–1892) was born into a family of Anglican clergyman and educated at Cambridge University. Although he completed much of his great work by 1842 (including "Ulysses"and "Morte d'Arthur"), he did not achieve fame until the 1840s. In 1833, his close friend Arthur Hallam died, which led Tennyson to produce a series of elegies; published in 1850 as *In Memoriam*, this collection is often considered his masterpiece. In 1850, Tennyson, for the first time financially secure, married Emily Sellwood after an engagement of almost fifteen years. Like many Victorians, Tennyson was deeply interested in developments in science, industry, and philosophy, but he was also very concerned about their uncertain moral and social implications. He was appointed Poet Laureate in 1850 and a Baron in 1884.

Robert Browning

Until his elopement with Elizabeth Barrett and their move to Italy in 1846, Robert Browning (1812–1889) was rarely absent from his parents' home, which included an extensive library. Although he published his first poem at age twenty-one, he did not achieve wide recognition until after his wife's death in 1861. His peak in productivity began after his arrival in Rome with Elizabeth and extended to approximately 1870. After his return to England, he became second only to Lord Tennyson in poetic popularity. When he died he was honored with burial in the Poet's Corner in Westminster Abbey. Although he wrote in many poetic forms, Browning is especially associated with the dramatic monologue, of which "My Last Duchess" is an example.

Walt Whitman

Born in Long Island, New York, Walt Whitman (1819–1892) moved at the age of four with his family to Brooklyn. Educated in public schools and later as a printer's apprentice, Whitman earned his living at several occupations, including teacher, printer, reporter, and editor. In 1855, he published *Leaves of Grass*. The volume did not sell well, and many of those who read or reviewed it found it distasteful in content and unpoetic in form. Whitman, however, found a champion in Ralph Waldo Emerson and a receptive audience abroad. During the Civil War, Whitman volunteered as a nurse for the Union cause and wrote America's most important and moving poems concerning the conflict, among them "Cavalry Crossing a Ford." In 1873, he suffered a stroke from which he never fully recovered, followed by a deep depression which descended after the death of his mother. By the end of his life, Whitman had become a legend. *Leaves of Grass*, issued in revised and augmented editions every few years throughout Whitman's life, marks a profound contribution to the liberation of American poetry. Experimenting with rhythms, Whitman freed his poetry from metric regularity while writing with extraordinary frankness about himself. Both practices rendered his poems very different from the popular genteel poetry of his day. "I sound my barbaric yawp over the roofs of the world," he wrote in "Song of Myself," and he seemed to challenge other poets to do the same.

Matthew Arnold

A son of a clergyman and headmaster, Matthew Arnold (1822–1888) earned his living primarily through his work in education. Arnold was an inspector of schools for thirty-five years, traveling extensively throughout England as part of his job. He also visited other European countries to study their systems of education. In 1857, he was elected to the Professorship of Poetry at Oxford, a part-time position that he held for ten years. His literary career falls neatly into four periods: in the 1850s he wrote poetry— "Dover Beach" was written during this time but published later; in the 1860s he wrote literary and social criticism; in the 1870s he wrote his religious and educational tracts; and in the 1880s he produced a second set of literary criticism. His poems are often meditative, melancholy, and concerned with spiritual alienation.

Christina Rossetti

Christina Rossetti's (1830–1894) father was an Italian political refugee, and her brother was the poet Dante Gabriel Rossetti. Christina was a devout High Anglican who dedicated her life to caring for relatives and doing good works for the church and charity. She broke off two engagements because, by her standards, neither man proved sufficiently devout. The apparent simplicity of many of her poems often masks complex emotional underpinnings. Many of her poems deal with painful breakups. Included in this text is one of her most famous poems, "Uphill," a religious allegory.

Emily Dickinson

Daughter of a lawyer who was elected to the United States Congress, Emily Dickinson (1830–1886) rarely left Amherst, Massachusetts. While she corresponded and met with friends, she tended to be reclusive, spending much of her time in her family home or in the garden. While she wrote nearly

1,800 poems, only 8 were published in her lifetime. Their posthumous publication in 1890 marks as significant an event for American letters as the publication of Whitman's *Leaves of Grass*. Dickinson's poetry is revolutionary in both form and content. While the themes she commonly treated—nature, death and dying, love, beauty, and her self—were typically "poetic," her unconventional treatment of them sets her apart from her literary progenitors. She typically uses the ballad stanza, irregular punctuation and capitalization, off- or slant-rhymes, almost clinically precise images, and a wide range of tones and moods.

Thomas Hardy

Thomas Hardy (1840–1928) was born in rural southwest England and went to London in 1861 to continue his studies and begin his career as an architect. His career as a writer did not begin until his second novel, *Under the Greenwood Tree* (1872), met with some success. After writing his last novel, *Jude the Obscure* (1896), and after publication of *The Dynasts* (1903–1908), his three-part epic-drama concerning the Napoleonic Wars, Hardy dedicated himself entirely to poetry. His poems, which frequently focus on a dramatic situation, often appear conventional, but his diction is distinctive, his rhythms not quite orthodox, and his convictions strong and often surprising.

Gerard Manley Hopkins

Educated at Oxford, Gerard Manley Hopkins (1844–1889) converted to Catholicism in 1866 and became a priest in 1877. As a Jesuit priest, Hopkins was devout and conscientious, serving several parishes throughout England and Scotland until his appointment as Chair of Classics at University College, Dublin. Hopkins subordinated his poetry to his priestly duties, with the result that none of his poems were published during his lifetime. His work first appeared in 1918, but it wasn't until a second publication in 1930 that it attracted widespread attention. His poetic experimentation made him seem a poet of the twentieth rather than the nineteenth century. His "sprung rhythm," for example, refers to an experimental, flexible rhythm with irregular stress patterns that sometimes pulsate and are often difficult to scan with certainty. While he wrote poems like "God's Grandeur" and "Pied Beauty," which celebrate God's presence in His creations, he also wrote the *Terrible Sonnets* (1885–1889), poems which depict desolation and self-doubt over his worthiness.

A. E. Housman

A renowned classical scholar, first at University College, London, and later at Cambridge, A. E. Housman (1859–1936) published only two volumes of poetry in his lifetime, *A Shropshire Lad* (1896), which became one of the most popular and bestselling books of verse in the English language, and *Last Poems* (1922); a third, *More Poems,* was published just after his death.

Housman's poetry is marked by irony and a sense of the brevity of youth and love; his unrequited love for Moses Jackson, a classmate at Oxford, is often seen as the inspiration for the frequently melancholy tone of *A Shropshire Lad* in particular. Formally, his verse is distinguished by its classical simplicity, epigrammatic force, and musicality.

William Butler Yeats

William Butler Yeats (1865–1939) was born in Dublin to moderately prosperous Protestant parents. His father was a lawyer turned artist. As a youth, Yeats spent his time between London, Dublin, and his mother's native county of Sligo. He eventually became the central figure in the Irish Literary Revival of the 1890s. He drew on Irish materials to build a foundation for his own work and to instill national pride in his fellow citizens. With Lady Gregory, he founded the Dublin Abbey Theatre, which he hoped would be the voice of modern Irish culture. While he was an accomplished writer of fiction, drama, literary criticism, essays, and autobiography, he was foremost a poet. He wrote poetry throughout his long life, but it is the work of his last twenty years that makes him one of the most important poets of the twentieth century. His poems are celebrated for their use of symbols and strong rhythms and the remarkable clarity of their imagery. Yeats won the Nobel Prize for Literature in 1923.

Edwin Arlington Robinson

Through his mother, Edwin Arlington Robinson (1869–1935) was a descendent of Anne Bradstreet. He grew up in Gardiner, Maine, and as a young man experienced significant physical and emotional distress: he suffered for years with a painful abscess of his ear, and he lost his fiancée to his brother, a loss which by his own account he never overcame. He dedicated his writing career exclusively to poetry, publishing his first volume, *The Torrent and the River* (1896) at his own expense. After receiving this volume from his son, President Theodore Roosevelt championed the poet and secured for him both a clerkship at the Custom House in New York and a contract from Scribner's. Robinson's poems abound with characters suffering isolation and existential despair. Like Robert Frost, Robinson insisted on the continued use of conventional verse forms and regular meters. Robinson earned the first of three Pulitzer Prizes for his *Collected Poems* (1921).

Paul Laurence Dunbar

Paul Laurence Dunbar (1872–1906) was born in Dayton, Ohio to parents who had both been slaves. Writing steadily while working as an elevator operator, Dunbar achieved celebrity when William Dean Howells reviewed *Majors and Minors* (1895), his second volume of poetry, and subsequently wrote the introduction to *Lyrics of Lowly Life* (1896). Dunbar was the first

African American to attempt to make his living solely by writing; he was one of the first to gain national prominence as a writer. Dunbar wrote not only poetry but also short stories, essays, and novels, in a short but prolific career: he published nineteen books in the last twelve years of his life. Dunbar's work was noted in particular for its incorporation of black dialect. The tone of these works tended toward the sentimental, though toward the end of his career they evidenced a trace of the bitterness and racial protest that characterizes much of the most significant African-American literature of the later twentieth century.

Robert Frost

Although Robert Frost (1874–1963) is closely associated with New England, he was actually born in San Francisco. After his father's death there in 1885, Frost's mother moved the family first to New Hampshire and then to Massachusetts. Frost eventually studied at both Darmouth and Harvard without taking a degree; he earned a living by teaching school and farming part time. In 1912, he moved to England with his wife and four children, there publishing his first important volumes of poetry, *A Boy's Will* (1913) and *North of Boston* (1914). By the time he returned to America in 1915, Frost was established as a poet. He settled with his family on a New Hampshire farm and while continuing to write verse at an astonishing pace, he taught at many colleges, including Amherst, Middlebury, Wesleyan, and Harvard. Frost won the first of four Pulitzer Prizes in 1924 and eventually became unquestionably the most popular American poet of the twentieth century. In 1955, a mountain in Vermont was named after him, and in 1961, he read at John F. Kennedy's presidential inauguration. Frost's poetry exhibits in some respects a link between the nineteenth and twentieth centuries; he insisted on traditional rhymes and metrical forms but rejected the florid language of the nineteenth-century Fireside poets. He wrote with precision, drawing on ordinary speech patterns and diction while dealing with dark themes of isolation, alienation, and death. For Frost, a poem "begins in delight and ends in wisdom" and represents "a momentary stay against confusion."

Amy Lowell

Born into wealth and privilege, Amy Lowell (1874–1925) was a descendant of poet James Russell Lowell and an ancestor of Robert Lowell. During World War I, she took over as leader of the Imagist movement when Ezra Pound, a strong influence, disassociated himself from it. Despite her association with Imagism, Lowell wrote in many styles, experimenting with rhythms both in meter and in free verse. She was a colorful figure—massively obese, scatological, and an habitual cigar smoker, Lowell once declared, "Lord, I'm a walking sideshow!"—and a much sought-after lecturer and reader. In addition to poetry, Lowell wrote criticism, translations, and a massive scholarly biography of John Keats (1925). "Patterns" (from *Men, Women, and Ghosts,* 1916) is an expression of outrage at the senselessness of war and the soul-killing constraints of the society that condones it.

Carl Sandburg

Carl Sandburg (1878–1967) was born into a poor family in Galesburg, Illinois. At thirteen, Sandburg was forced to leave school. For the next several years, he worked a variety of jobs in various towns throughout the Midwest. In 1898, he served in the Spanish-American War and afterwards returned to the Midwest to attend Lombard College. In 1908, Sandburg married, and in 1910, he worked as secretary to the mayor of Milwaukee before joining the editorial staff of the *Milwaukee Ledger*. In 1913, he went to Chicago, where he established himself as a journalist, editorialist, columnist, and poet. With *Smoke and Steel* (1920), Sandburg secured his rising reputation as a poet of the common people. In the following years, Sandburg toured the country, reading his poems and singing folk songs to his own accompaniment on guitar. He continued to write newspaper columns, while also writing nature books, a novel, children's books, commentaries on World War II, and a massive six-volume biography on Abraham Lincoln. He won Pulitzer Prizes for *Abraham Lincoln: The War Years* (4 volumes, 1939) and for *Collected Poems* (1950).

Wallace Stevens

Born in Reading, Pennsylvania, Wallace Stevens (1879–1955) was a successful lawyer and insurance executive who wrote some of the most influential poetry of the twentieth century. His first volume of poems, *Harmonium* (1923), was not published until he was forty-four years old. At the time, it attracted little attention, and Stevens, with increased corporate responsibilities, published little over the next decade. After *Harmonium* was reprinted in 1931 to a far better reception, Stevens began to write steadily. His *Collected Poems* (1954), for which he received the Pulitzer Prize and National Book Award, established his reputation as a major American poet. Stevens's complex poetry can be many things simultaneously: elegant and bizarre, playful and meditative, abstract and sensual. Among his concerns are perceptions and the perceiver, reality and the imagination, and the real and the ideal.

William Carlos Williams

William Carlos Williams (1883–1963) studied in several European cities and met with American modernists living in Europe, but soon returned to the United States, ultimately concluding that richer poetic materials could be found at home. He spent most of his remaining life in Rutherford, New Jersey, where he was born. From 1910 on, Williams practiced medicine, and he drew on the lives of his poor and middle-class patients for his short stories and poems. To represent American speech patterns in poetry, he experimented with what he called "the variable line," a rhythm not regulated by the number of syllables or by their distinction as "long" or "short." While he is a poet of ideas, he insists on "the concrete particular," drawing his imagery from everyday objects and situations. *Pater-*

son (1946), his long poem in five books, represents the culmination of his work. Weaving together materials from newspapers, letters, documents, and interviews with lyrical and descriptive passages, Williams presents a portrait of the New Jersey city from its Indian origins to its industrial present. *Paterson*, like almost all of Williams's work, resonates with larger implications about the American experience.

Elinor Wylie

Elinor Wylie (1885–1928), poet and novelist, was born into a prominent political and social family in Pennsylvania. In 1910, she was ostracized from her social world when she deserted her husband and child and eloped with Horace Wylie, a prominent lawyer. In 1921 Wylie published *Nets to Catch the Wind*, the first of her verse collections to bear her name. This volume contains some of her most celebrated verse, which bore strong traces of influence by the Metaphysical and Elizabethan poets, and drew widespread praise for its striking imagery and its mastery of rhyme and meter. Wylie's work tends to reflect her traditional and privileged background; it provides one measure of the tremendous changes experienced by Americans in the aftermath of World War I. Divorced from her second husband in 1923, Wylie married poet William Rose Benét later that year. Her last eight years were spent in a flurry of activity, writing poetry, short stories, novels, and criticism and editing two literary magazines.

Ezra Pound

Ezra Pound (1885–1972) was born in Hailey, Idaho, and raised in a suburb of Philadelphia. Educated at Hamilton College and the University of Pennsylvania, Pound left for Europe in 1908 and spent most of the rest of his life there. Pound generated a firestorm of controversy as a result of his public support for Mussolini and the radio broadcasts he made in support of the Fascists during World War II. He was arrested for treason in 1943 and remanded to St. Elizabeth's Hospital for the Criminally Insane, where he spent some thirteen years before his release and return to Europe. It is hard to overstate Pound's influence on modernism. He served as an advisor or editor to a number of major authors, including T. S. Eliot, James Joyce, W. B. Yeats, Marianne Moore, William Carlos Williams, and H. D. (Hilda Doolittle). He was the leader of the pre-World War I Imagist movement, which endorsed a minimalist approach to poetry, advocating the use of precise imagery over verbal embellishments: "In a Station of the Metro," first published in *Personae* (1909), is an example of an Imagist poem. Following the Imagist years, Pound advocated for "the poem including history": the culmination of this stage of his poetic development were the *Cantos* (I–XVI published 1925, with 100 more following in various editions). Epic in scope, the *Cantos* interweave major events and figures in Western and Eastern culture, pillory philistines, the moneyed interests, and war machines and proffer ideas for the establishment of a new society.

H. D. (Hilda Doolittle)

Hilda Doolittle (1886–1961) was born into a socially prominent family in Bethlehem, Pennsylvania. Her mother was an artist and musician and her father a professor of astronomy. Doolittle met and fell in love with Ezra Pound in 1905, when she was still in her teens; her family intervened, putting an end to the affair, but Doolittle dropped out of Bryn Mawr in her sophomore year and, in 1911, she went to Europe, moving in the same literary circles frequented by Pound. H. D. is known primarily for her Imagist poetry; "Heat," first published in *Sea Garden* (1916), is one of her finest Imagist poems. She continued to write experimental poetry and fiction throughout her life, and, in 1960, she became the first woman to receive the prestigious Award of Merit Medal for Poetry from the American Academy of Arts and Letters.

Marianne Moore

Born in St. Louis, Marianne Moore (1887–1972) was educated at Bryn Mawr in Pennsylvania. In 1918, Moore and her mother settled in New York City, where she lived for the rest of her life. From 1925 to 1929 Moore served as acting editor of *The Dial*, the journal in which many of the seminal works of modernist poetry were first published. Known for her acute skills of observation, Moore wrote "objectivist" poetry, so called for its especially detailed, compact, and reflective portraits of precisely delineated subjects. Moore's work is notable for its wit and intellectual appeal, though it also has broad popular appeal. Her first volume, *Poems* (1921), was published without her knowledge by H. D. and Robert McAlmon. Her *Collected Poems* (1951) was awarded both a Pulitzer and the Bollingen Prize. Baseball fans might be interested to hear that Moore, herself an avid fan, threw out the first ball at the season opener at Yankee Stadium in 1968.

T. S. Eliot

A descendant of a prominent New England family, Thomas Stearns Eliot (1888–1965) was born in St. Louis, Missouri. Eliot studied literature and philosophy at Harvard; he also studied at the Sorbonne and Oxford. From World War I, he lived almost his entire adult life abroad. In 1918, he worked as a bank clerk at Lloyd's Bank in London, and in 1925 he accepted a position as a director at the British publishing firm of Faber & Faber, where he worked for the rest of his life. He came to prominence with the publication of *Prufrock and Other Observations* in 1917. "The Love Song of J. Alfred Prufrock" is often regarded as the first major modernist poem, with its recurring and aggregate images and juxtapositions, its rhythmic variation and precision, and its sense of irony, despair, and alienation. With the publication of *The Waste Land* in 1922, Eliot became the most influential poet and critic writing in English, a distinction which lasted at least until World War II. In 1948, Eliot won the Nobel Prize for Literature.

Claude McKay

A Jamaican immigrant, Claude McKay (1889–1948) was one of the most militant artists of the Harlem Renaissance. McKay's *Home to Harlem* (1928), the story of a black soldier's disillusionment on returning home after World War I, became the first national bestseller written by an African American. Apart from this work, McKay is best known for his protest verse, which expresses outrage at America's racism. Perhaps surprisingly given the content of his poems, McKay, like Countee Cullen, preferred traditional verse forms. "America," first published in book form in *Harlem Shadows* (1922), takes the form of an English sonnet, providing an interesting example of this marriage of radical politics and conservative aesthetics.

John Crowe Ransom

Son of a Methodist minister, John Crowe Ransom (1888–1974) was born in Pulaski, Tennessee. He entered Vanderbilt University at fifteen and went on to study at Oxford as a Rhodes Scholar. In 1914, he returned to teach at Vanderbilt but soon left to serve with the United States Army in World War I. In 1922, Ransom and several other Southern writers, including Allen Tate, Donald Davidson, and Robert Penn Warren, formed a group called the Fugitives. Their influential magazine, *The Fugitive* (1922–1925), signaled the literary renaissance of the American South. The Fugitives considered themselves "classical modernists," meaning they produced classical forms of art with modernist sensibilities. Later, these same writers formed a group called the Agrarians, who argued for traditional Southern values without racism, as a response to the rampant industrialism of the era. In 1937 Ransom left Vanderbilt for Kenyon College, where he founded and edited the *Kenyon Review*. His students included Robert Lowell, Randall Jarrell, and Peter Taylor. In 1951, Ransom was awarded the Bollingen Prize in Poetry for the body of his work. He published his third edition of *Selected Poems* in 1969 and *Beating the Bushes*, a volume of essays, in 1971.

Edna St. Vincent Millay

Born in Rockland, Maine, Edna St. Vincent Millay (1892–1950) always considered herself a writer. She published her first poem at age twelve, and after attending Barnard and graduating from Vassar College in 1917, she published her first collection of poems. She moved to Greenwich Village and quickly established a poetic reputation, winning the Pulitzer Prize in 1923 for *The Harp-Weaver and Other Poems*. An independent woman of the Jazz Age, she attacked conventional expectations of female behavior. After her marriage in 1923, she settled on a farm in Austerlitz, New York, where she wrote some of her finest poems. Her later writings are more political than the earlier poems; in the 1930s, she joined with other writers to voice her opposition to rising European fascism and freely used her poetry to broadcast her views. Millay wrote little in the last decade of her life. Her *Collected Poems* were published posthumously in 1956.

Archibald MacLeish

Born in the Chicago suburb of Glencoe, Archibald MacLeish (1892–1982) graduated from Yale and then Harvard Law School. He combined a very active and diverse public career with a dedication to poetry. MacLeish served in World War I, practiced law in Boston while teaching constitutional law at Harvard, lived with his wife and two children in Paris for five years, worked as an editor of *Fortune* magazine, served as Librarian of Congress, and was appointed Assistant Secretary of State before returning to Harvard to teach rhetoric and oratory. In 1958, he wrote a hit play, the verse drama entitled *J. B.*, which won a Pulitzer Prize and a Tony Award. He also won Pulitzers for his volume of poems *Conquistador* (1932) and his *Collected Poems* (1953).

Wilfred Owen

Perhaps the best of the poets writing in and about World War I, Wilfred Owen (1893–1918) studied at London University and enlisted in the English army at the outbreak of the war. He fought in the Battle of the Somme, was decorated for bravery, and was later hospitalized for shell shock. He returned to the front after recuperating, only to be killed a week before the Armistice. At least in part while in the trenches, Owen wrote technically experimental poems that describe both the suffering and what he called the "pity" inherent in war. Owen published only four poems in his lifetime. Owen was unknown until Siegfried Sassoon, another poet whom he had met in an army hospital, published Owen's *Poems* in 1920.

Dorothy Parker

Born Dorothy Rothschild, Parker (1893–1967) was raised in New York City. In 1916 Parker became an editor at *Vogue* and later moved to *Vanity Fair*. She was a celebrated wit and leading member of the notorious "Algonquin Round Table," a collection of writers and other intellectuals who met regularly at the Algonquin Hotel in New York throughout the 1920s and early 1930s. Parker's reviews, essays, short stories, and poems were published frequently but irregularly in *The New Yorker* from 1926 through 1955. Her poems, including "Résumé," were first collected in *Enough Rope* (1926); her poetry tends to be witty, sardonic, and light. Her short stories were first collected in *After Such Pleasures* (1932) and *Here Lies* (1939). With her second husband, Alan Campbell, Parker moved in the 1950s to Hollywood, where she collaborated on a number of film scripts, among them *A Star Is Born* (1937).

E. E. Cummings

Edward Estlin Cummings (1894–1962) was born in Cambridge, Massachusetts. His father was a prominent Harvard English professor and Unitarian minister in Boston. In 1917, after earning his M.A. at Harvard, Cummings went to France to serve as a volunteer ambulance driver for the Red Cross in World War I. A series of complications led to his being briefly imprisoned for espionage, an episode in his life detailed in his autobiographical novel, *The Enormous Room* (1922); President Woodrow Wilson personally intervened to have him released. Cummings studied painting in France after the war and joined other American expatriates who lived in Paris in the 1920s. Modernist experiments in the visual arts proved a large influence on Cummings's poems, the first volume of which was *Tulips and Chimneys* (1923). His poetry is individualistic, playful, and technically experimental, in particular for its eccentric use of typography and punctuation. It is also known for its extensive use of slang, dialect, and the rhythms of jazz. Interestingly, Cummings is both a passionate love poet and a caustic satirist, especially opposed to war and forces that impose conformity and hinder deep human feeling.

Jean Toomer

Eugene Pinchback Toomer (1894–1967) was born into a broken home in Washington, D.C. He lived with his maternal grandfather and his mother until her remarriage in 1906, when he went with his mother and stepfather to live in New Rochelle, New York. Toomer attended several different colleges but never took a degree. In 1919, he decided to become a writer. *Cane*, his most important work and the source for the poems included in this anthology, was published in 1923. The book, which combines prose and poetry, grew out of his encounters with rural African-American culture on a trip to the South. The book was widely celebrated upon publication and remains Toomer's greatest artistic achievement. Toomer's heritage was a source of controversy and frustration for him. Light-complexioned, he had a small amount of African-American blood inherited from his grandfather. Many accused him of denying his African-American heritage, but he refused to speak for African Americans in his writing, declaring "I am of no race. I am of the human race."

Langston Hughes

"I explain and illuminate the Negro condition in America. This applies to 90 percent of my work," declared Langston Hughes (1902–1967). Born in Joplin, Missouri, and raised in Lawrence, Kansas, and Cleveland, Ohio, Hughes evolved into one of the most original, versatile, and prolific authors of African-American literature. He wrote poetry, drama, fiction, essays, autobiography, songs, opera libretti, children's books, and a history of the NAACP. In all, he produced more than sixty books: perhaps best known are the early verse collection *The Weary Blues* (1926); *Mulatto* (1935), a play; and his two volumes of autobiography, *The Big Sea* (1940) and *I Wonder As I Wander* (1954). Hughes was a dominant voice in twentieth-century American literature and the century's most influential African-American poet, serving as a model for poets like Gwendolyn Brooks and playwrights like Lorraine Hansberry.

Countee Cullen

The adopted son of the minister of an African Methodist church in Harlem, Countee Porter Cullen (1903–1946) received degrees from both New York University and Harvard. By his second year in college, he was publishing poems in major literary magazines. His first book, *Color* (1925), appeared when he was a senior in college. While he wrote throughout his life, he was most successful, artistically and commercially, before he was thirty. He later supported himself as a junior high school teacher in New York. He wrote most often about the African-American experience, and he, like Claude McKay, favored traditional verse forms.

W. H. Auden

Born in York, England, Wystan Hugh Auden (1907–1973) was the central figure of a group of left-wing intellectuals who in the 1930s perceived depression-era England as a victim of its antiquated economic and social systems. Auden served in the Spanish Civil War; a number of his most famous poems stem from that experience. Though an early advocate of socialism, Auden turned to Christianity during World War II: his poetry reflected the shift. In 1939, Auden immigrated to the United States, and, in 1946, he became a U.S. citizen. In 1956, he became a professor of poetry at Oxford, his alma mater. His poetry, especially his early work, is often informed by his social consciousness, and while it tends toward the didactic, its tone is often relieved by an irreverent sense of humor. "Musée des Beaux Arts" is a meditation inspired by a painting by Pieter Brueghel.

Theodore Roethke

Theodore Roethke (1908–1963) was born in Saginaw, Michigan, where his domineering father ran a successful floral business. Perhaps unsurprisingly, images of authoritative, masculine figures and flowering plants are pervasive in his poetry. Roethke's adult life was marked by emotional illness and alcoholism. Educated at the University of Michigan, Roethke taught at several colleges before settling at the University of Washington in 1947. He won a Pulitzer Prize for *The Waking* (1953) and a National Book Award and Bollingen Prize for *Words for the Wind* (1958). Poet John Berryman characterized Roethke's work as "teutonic, irregular, delicate, botanical, psychological, irreligious, [and] personal."

Elizabeth Bishop

Born in Worcester, Massachusetts, Elizabeth Bishop (1911–1979) had a very difficult childhood. Her father died when she was eight months old, and her mother was permanently institutionalized when Bishop was only four. She struggled throughout her life with asthma, which left her isolated as a child and shy as an adult. After attending Vassar College,

Bishop spent much of her life in the tropics, first in Key West and then in Brazil. She corresponded frequently with poets Robert Lowell and Marianne Moore, who was Bishop's mentor and confidante. Her poems are characterized by her precise powers of observation, her conversational tone, and an almost mystical movement to a symbolic resolution. She won a Pulitzer Prize for *Poems* (1956) and a National Book Award for *The Complete Poems* (1969).

Robert Hayden

Born Asa Bundy Sheffey in the slums of Detroit, Michigan, Robert Hayden (1913–1980) was very young when his parents divorced. His mother left him with foster parents, who gave him their name and raised him. Hayden described himself as "divided," and his poems (the first of which he published at the age of eighteen) often concern self-conflict. As a youth, Hayden was introverted and spent many hours reading and writing. Educated at Detroit City College (now Wayne State University) and the University of Michigan, he worked for the Federal Writers Project of the WPA in the late 1930s. He went on to teach at Fisk University and the University of Michigan. Hayden draws both from personal experience and from the lives of such historical figures as Nat Turner, Harriet Tubman, and Malcolm X in his poetry, but he steadfastly resisted identification as an "ethnic" poet, insisting always that his poetry was universal.

John Frederick Nims

Born in Muskegon, Michigan, John Frederick Nims (1913–1999) received his M.A. from the University of Notre Dame and his Ph.D. from the University of Chicago. In addition to eight volumes of poetry, he published a number of translations (*The Poems of St. John of the Cross*, 1979; *The Complete Poems of Michelangelo*, 2000), edited anthologies (*Western Wind: An Introduction to Poetry*), and edited *Poetry* magazine from 1978 to 1984. The recipient of numerous awards for his poetry, he taught at several universities, including Harvard, Notre Dame, the University of Toronto, the University of Florence, the University of Florida, the University of Illinois at Urbana, and the University of Illinois at Chicago.

William Stafford

William Stafford (1914–1993) was born and raised in Hutchinson, Kansas, earned a Ph.D. at the University of Iowa, and taught for many years at Lewis and Clark College in Oregon. The landscapes of these places inform much of his poetry. His poems are quiet and poised, conversational, and solidly constructed. Although he had published many poems previously in periodicals and anthologies, his first volume of poetry was not published until 1960, and he first received widespread recognition with his third volume, *Traveling through the Dark* (1962).

Dylan Thomas

Dylan Thomas (1914–1953) was born in the Welsh seaport of Swansea, where his formal education began and ended at Swansea Grammar School. With the publication of *Eighteen Poems,* his first volume, in 1934, Thomas achieved widespread and immediate fame. His lyrical poetry features vivid metaphors, Christian and Freudian imagery, puns, and intricate patterns of sound, yet it tends to be more immediately accessible and emotional than many of the moderns' works. His colorful personality and melodious speaking voice made his reading tours the most successful of any poet in the century. While on his third American reading tour, Thomas died in New York City after a reckless drinking binge.

Randall Jarrell

A teacher, critic, and poet, Randall Jarrell (1914–1965) was born in Nashville, Tennessee, and spent his early years in California before returning to Nashville at age twelve. After demonstrating no interest in the business career his family had arranged for him, he enrolled at Vanderbilt University, studied under John Crowe Ransom, and edited a literary magazine. After graduating with an M.A., he taught English at Kenyon College, the University of Texas, and, after military service, the University of North Carolina. Jarrell published six volumes of poetry, a novel, and four volumes of criticism. "The Death of the Ball Turrett Gunner" is inspired by his experience in the air force during World War II.

John Berryman

Born in McAlester, Oklahoma, as John Smith, John Berryman (1914–1972) was the son of a schoolteacher and prosperous banker. The family moved to Florida when he was ten, and shortly after, his father committed suicide. Berryman and his mother moved to New York, where she remarried. Berryman was educated at Columbia University and Oxford, and he later taught at Harvard, Princeton, the University of Iowa's Writer's Workshop, and the University of Minnesota. While his career was successful, he suffered throughout his life from alcoholism, mental illness, and marital problems. For the 1969 publication of *The Dream Songs*, Berryman won a National Book Award and the Bollingen Prize. Poems in *The Dreams Songs* are generally considered confessional, despite the deployment of "Henry," the antihero of the sequence. The poems demonstrate a wide emotional range and can shift suddenly from gloomy introspection to whimsy.

Gwendolyn Brooks

Gwendolyn Brooks (1917–2000) was born in Topeka, Kansas but grew up on Chicago's South Side. Her first collection of poetry, *A Street in Bronzeville,* was published to critical praise in 1945, and her second volume, *Annie Allen,* won a Pulitzer Prize in 1950. Her later poetry, particularly that of the mid- to late 1960s, is more socially conscious and experimental than her earlier poetry. Of her later poetry, she once said that she wrote for "not just the blacks who go to college but also those who have their customary habitat in taverns and the street. . . . Anything I write is going to issue from a concern with and interest in blackness and its progress."

Robert Lowell

Born in Boston, Robert Lowell (1917–1977) was descended from a distinguished New England family that traced its roots from the Mayflower and through nineteenth-century poet James Russell Lowell and twentieth-century poet Amy Lowell. Robert Lowell studied at Harvard but graduated from Kenyon College, where he studied under John Crowe Ransom. Lowell's life was dedicated to the writing, teaching, and criticism of poetry. His work was interrupted, however, by emotional breakdowns that required hospitalization. In 1947, he won a Pulitzer Prize for *Lord Weary's Castle*, but his most influential work came more than a decade later. *Life Studies* (1959) was a daring and candid collection of self-exploration and self-exposure that marked the advent of "confessional poetry." *For the Union Dead* (1964) took its materials less from self-examination and more from historical New England, but it is invested with the same emotional intensity as his earlier work. In both collections, Lowell emphasizes the importance of poetic voice over structure. In the late 1960s, Lowell became increasingly more political, taking an active role in the movement to protest the Vietnam War. His last work, *Day by Day*, was published shortly before his death.

Richard Wilbur

Richard Wilbur (1921–) was born in New York City but spent much of his life in New England. He graduated from Amherst College and took his M.A. at Harvard. Wilbur taught at Harvard, Wellesley College, and Wesleyan University, where he remained for twenty years. Later he was a poet-in-residence at Smith College, and in 1987, he was appointed Poet Laureate of the United States. He served overseas during World War II. In 1957, his third book of poetry, *Things of This World*, brought him a Pulitzer Prize and a National Book Award. He won a second Pulitzer in 1989 for his *New and Collected Poems*. His poetry is noted for its precise and fresh imagery and its tightly controlled structures and rhythms. Wilbur thinks of a poem as an art object created not as a means of communication but as a self-contained experience of language, rhythm, and image.

Philip Larkin

Born in Coventry, England, to a working-class family, Philip Larkin (1922–1985) was educated at Oxford University and served for many years as a librarian in the provincial city of Hull. His first published work was a Yeatsian volume of poems, *The North Ship* (1946). After writing two novels, *Jill* (1946) and *A Girl in Winter* (1947), Larkin concentrated solely on verse. His collection *The Less Deceived* (1955) established Larkin as a lead-ing figure of the Movement poets, whose reaction against neo-Romantic poetry came to prominence in England in the 1950s. Larkin's poems are known for their control, thoughtfulness, wit, and irony. Less well known is the fact that Larkin was a great enthusiast for American jazz, publishing *All What Jazz*, a collection of record reviews, in 1970.

Allen Ginsberg

Allen Ginsberg (1926–1997) was born in Newark, New Jersey, where his father was a high school teacher and poet. After graduating from Colum-bia University, Ginsberg worked odd jobs while becoming an integral part of the Beat movement. In 1956, he achieved notoriety with the controver-sial *Howl and Other Poems*. Influenced primarily by William Blake's prophetic poems and by Walt Whitman, Ginsberg experimented in his verse with line length, rhythms, and diction. He lived a public life, active in the antiwar, civil rights, and other anti-establishment movements, and he was a lifelong advocate for alternative lifestyles.

John Ashbery

John Ashbery (1927–) was born in Rochester, New York. At Harvard, he met Frank O'Hara and Kenneth Koch, poets who moved with Ashbery to New York City and came to form the core of the "New York School" of poetry. Ashbery attended graduate school at Columbia and New York Uni-versity, and he worked at Oxford University Press and McGraw-Hill. In 1956, he received a Fulbright Fellowship, which gave him an opportunity to live in France, where he began his career as an art journalist. In 1965, Ashbery returned to New York and became Executive Editor of *Art News*. In 1974, he joined the faculty of Brooklyn College, where he remained until his retirement. He served as poetry editor of *Partisan Review* in 1976 and an art critic and editor at *Newsweek* beginning in 1980. Ashbery's work is unconventional, complex, and at times obscure. A restless experimenter with forms, he has written poems of one line and poems of two hundred pages (*Flow Chart*, 1991). Ashbery has won virtually all the major literary awards, including a Pulitzer Prize and National Book Award.

James Wright

James Wright (1927–1980) was born in Martins Ferry, Ohio, and educated at Kenyon College, the University of Vienna, and the University of Wash-ington, where he earned his Ph.D., afterwards teaching at the University of Minnesota, Macalester College, and Hunter College. In the 1950s, his poet-ry was relatively formal, but in the 1960s, it became more open, with con-versational diction and rhythm and varying line lengths. At this time, Wright was identified with Robert Bly as one of the leading exponents of the"deep image," a concept that argued for the image as the central fact of the poem and found mystical "deep" powers in images from the subconscious, dreams, and hallucinations. After the publication of his *Collected Poems* in 1971, Wright was awarded the Pulitzer Prize for poetry.

Anne Sexton

Anne Sexton (1928–1974) commented on poetry: "I think it should be a shock to the senses. It should almost hurt." Her confessional poems often reveal a self in torment and despair, and do indeed often shock and pain the reader with their blunt, unsparing revelations. Born in Newton, Massachusetts, Sexton began writing poetry in 1957, studying first under Maxine Kumin and, later, under Robert Lowell. By that time, she had eloped, given birth to two children, and attempted suicide. By writing so intimately about her own experiences as a wife, mother, and woman, she voiced the despair that confronted many women of her generation. A well-honored poet and full professor at Boston University, Sexton received numerous awards, including the Pulitzer Prize in 1967 for *Live or Die*. She committed suicide in 1974.

Gary Snyder

Born in San Francisco and raised on a small farm north of Seattle, Washington, Gary Snyder (1930–) graduated from Reed College and studied Japanese and Chinese culture at the University of California at Berkley. Associated with the Beat poets in the 1950s, he found inspiration and spirituality in Buddhism, Asian poetry, the culture of the American Indian, and nature. He spent much of his time from the mid-1950s until the 1970s living and writing in Japan. With his lifelong interest in hiking and camping, Snyder, in his poetry and his political convictions, is an advocate for environmental awareness. He won a Pulitzer Prize in 1975 for *Turtle Island*.

Linda Pastan

Linda Pastan (1932–) was born in New York City and educated at Radcliffe College and Brandeis University. She is the author of ten books of poetry, the most recent of which, *Carnival Evening: New and Selected Poems, 1968–1999*, was a finalist for a National Book Award. Pastan is a former Poet Laureate of Maryland, where she currently lives.

Sylvia Plath

Sylvia Plath (1932–1963) studied at Smith College and as an undergraduate won a prestigious award from *Mademoiselle*, working on the magazine's college board for a month in New York City. She afterward returned home and suffered an emotional breakdown, which led to a suicide attempt; *The Bell Jar* (1963) is her fictional account of this struggle. She eventually returned to Smith, graduated *summa cum laude*, and left for England to study at Cambridge on a Fulbright Fellowship. In England, she married the poet Ted Hughes, and the couple returned to the United States in 1957. After teaching at Smith for a year, Plath settled with Hughes in Boston, where she studied under Robert Lowell and became friends with Anne Sexton. The couple returned to England in 1959. In 1960, they had the first of two children, and Plath published *The Colossus*, her first collection of poetry. In 1962 the couple separated, and on February 11, 1963, Plath committed suicide. Her fame came posthumously, with the publication of *Ariel* (1965), *Crossing the Water* (1971), and *Winter Trees* (1972); in 1982 her *Collected Poems* won a Pulitzer Prize. Her poetry, insistent on metaphor and frequently confessional in mode, is equally capable of intense expressions of anguish and of dark humor.

Mark Strand

Born in Prince Edward Island, Canada, Mark Strand (1934–) graduated from Antioch College, studied painting under Josef Albers at Yale, and, after a year in Italy, studied at the University of Iowa Writer's Workshop. In addition to poetry, he has published translations, short stories, criticism, and children's stories, and he has edited several volumes of poetry. His poems are frequently stark and seemingly simple, but they are complicated by elements of surrealism that inform the imagery. In 1990, he was appointed Poet Laureate of the United States, and in 1999, he won the Pulitzer Prize for Poetry for *Blizzard of One* (1998).

Mary Oliver

Mary Oliver (1935–) was born in Cleveland and educated at Ohio State University and Vassar College. She has written ten volumes of poetry, of which *American Primitive* won the Pulitzer Prize in 1984 and *New and Selected Poems* received a National Book Award in 1992. She has also written three books of prose, including *A Handbook for Writing and Reading Metrical Verse* (1998). Her poems frequently move from observation to careful scrutiny and, ultimately, to deeper awareness or epiphany.

Lucille Clifton

Born in DePew, New York, Lucille Clifton (1936–) was educated at Howard University and Fredonia State Teachers' College. She published her first collection of verse, *Good Times*, in 1969. Clifton has taught at several universities and currently teaches creative writing at the University of California, Santa Cruz. "I am a Black woman poet," she has said, "and I sound like one." In addition to seven volumes of poetry, Clifton has written fifteen children's books expressly for an African-American audience, including an award-winning series featuring events in the life of an African-American boy, Everett Anderson.

Marge Piercy

Marge Piercy (1936–), author of novels, short stories, plays, poetry, essays, and science fiction, was born in Detroit, Michigan. Educated at the University of Michigan and at Northwestern University, Piercy has held posts at numerous colleges and universities, including the State University of New York at Buffalo, Vanderbilt University, and the University of Michigan. Piercy's commitment to social causes has been evidenced in her participation in numerous political and civic organizations, including, in the 1960s, the radical Students for a Democratic Society. Her identity as a Jewish woman and a feminist has informed much of her art. Her latest books are *The Art of Blessing the Day: Poems with a Jewish Theme*; *Early Grrrl: The Early Poems of Marge Piercy*; and the novel *Three Women*, all published in 1999.

Margaret Atwood

Margaret Atwood (1939–), one of Canada's foremost writers, was born in Ottawa. Because her father was a forest entomologist, she spent a large part of her childhood living in the Canadian wilderness, where she entertained herself by reading and writing. She graduated from the University of Toronto and received an M.A. from Radcliffe College in 1962. The recipient of many prestigious awards and fellowships, Atwood has won international acclaim for her fiction, poetry, and criticism. Notable publications include *The Circle Game* (1962), a collection of poems; *Bluebeard's Egg* (1983), a short story collection; the novel *The Handmaid's Tale* (1986); and the recent *The Blind Assassin* (2000). Atwood currently resides in Toronto.

Seamus Heaney

Robert Lowell has called Seamus Heaney (1939–) "the most important Irish poet since Yeats." Born just northwest of Belfast, Heaney was educated at Queen's College and St. Joseph's College, both in the city. He published his first collection, *Eleven Poems*, in 1965. In addition to several volumes of poetry, he has published essay collections and translations, including a widely heralded translation of the Old English epic *Beowulf* (2000). He has taught at many colleges, including Carysfort College (Dublin), the University of California at Berkeley, Harvard, and Oxford. His poetry has retained its roots in the Irish soil, but he elegantly extends his themes to larger issues of history, culture, and identity. In 1995, Heaney was awarded the Nobel Prize in Literature. The citation praised him "for work of lyrical beauty and ethical depth, which exalt everyday miracles and the living past."

Sharon Olds

Sharon Olds (1942–) was born in San Francisco, raised, as she said, a "hellfire Calvinist." Educated at Stanford University and Columbia University, she published *Satan Says*, her first volume of poetry, in 1980. Her second volume, *The Dead and the Living*, won a Lamont Poetry Prize in 1983; it combines "public" poems inspired by historical portraits with "private" poems inspired by family members and friends. "The One Girl at the Boys' Party" is from this collection. She currently teaches in the Graduate Creative Writing Program at New York University and helps run the NYU Workshop Program at Goldwater Hospital on Roosevelt Island, New York. *Blood, Tin, Straw*, her latest volume of poems, was published in 1999.

Louise Glück

Louise Glück (1943–) studied with the Confessional poets (of whom John Berryman, Sylvia Plath, and Anne Sexton were leading practioners), but kept her distance from their poetic practice. In such volumes as *The House on Marshland* (1975), Glück writes about birth, family life, sex, and motherhood, but her poetry tends to have a distant quality that echoes her preoccupation with the themes of alienation and powerlessness in an indifferent universe.

Yusef Komunyakaa

Born in Bogalusa, Louisiana, Yusef Komunyakaa (1947–) enlisted in the army soon after graduating from high school and served several tours of duty in Vietnam. Upon his return, he earned an undergraduate degree at the University of Colorado, an M.A. at Colorado State University, and an M.F.A. in creative writing at the University of California. His poetry frequently draws from jazz and R&B music. "Facing It" is the final poem in *Dien Cai Dau* (1988), his collection of poems about Vietnam. Komunyakaa currently teaches at Princeton.

Leslie Marmon Silko

A Native American, Leslie Marmon Silko (1948–) was brought up in Laguna Pueblo, New Mexico. She has taught at the University of Arizona and the University of New Mexico, and she has been honored with a MacArthur Fellowship. Her essays, poems, and stories center on the traditions of the Navajo people; they celebrate Native-American culture and traditions, especially a respect for the land and for the past. Her books include *Ceremony* (1970), her first novel; *Storyteller* (1981), a collection of tribal folktales, family anecdotes, photographs, poems, and stories; *The Almanac of the Dead* (1993); and *Second Water* (1993), a collection of poems.

Timothy Steele

"I believe that our ability to organize thought and speech into measure is one of the most precious endowments of the human race," says Timothy Steele (1948–), an ardent practitioner and defender of traditional verse forms. He has also said that "metrical tradition is the trunk of the great tree of poetry." Born in Burlington, Vermont, Steele graduated from Stanford University and earned his Ph.D. at Brandeis University. He has written several volumes of poetry, including *Sapphics and Uncertainties: Poems 1970–1986* and *The Color Wheel* (1994); critical works such as *Missing Measures: Modern Poetry and the Revolt Against Meter* (1990); and *All the Fun's in How You Say a Thing* (1999), a prosody handbook. He teaches at California State University, Los Angeles.

Carolyn Forché

Born in Detroit, Michigan, Carolyn Forché (1950–) graduated from Michigan State University and received an M.F.A. from Bowling Green State University. She has published three books of poems, including *The Country Between Us* (1982), from which "The Colonel" is taken. *The Country Between Us* was inspired by Forché's several extended trips to El Salvador between 1978 and 1980, trips which she said transformed her life as she documented human rights violations for Amnesty International. In El Salvador she worked closely with Monsignor Oscar Romero, the Archbishop of San Salvador who was assassinated in 1980. Romero asked Forché to return to the United States to tell the world about the human atrocities in his country, which request she says she has tried to honor through her volume of poetry and her numerous speaking and reading engagements. In an age when poetry is generally concerned with the individual, Forché's poetry, from her first volume *Gathering the Tribes* (1976), has been concerned with the community. She currently teaches at George Mason University in Virginia.

Joy Harjo

Born in Tulsa, Oklahoma, Joy Harjo (1951–) is a member of the Creek tribe. She was educated at the University of New Mexico and at the Iowa Writer's Workshop. She has published several volumes of poetry, including *In Mad Love and War* (1990), the volume that includes "Eagle Poem," a poem-prayer that gives thanks for life and asks that beauty be central to our existence. Harjo's poetry frequently combines realistic description with Native-American spirituality. She currently teaches at the University of New Mexico.

Rita Dove

Born in Akron, Ohio, Rita Dove (1952–) graduated from Miami University of Ohio, studied for a year in Germany on a Fulbright, and then attended the Iowa Writer's Workshop, where she met her husband, the writer Fred Viebahn, and earned her M.F.A. in 1977. Her first published collection was *The Yellow House on the Corner* (1980), closely followed by *Museum* (1983) and *Thomas and Beulah* (1986), a loosely structured sequence inspired by the lives of her grandparents. The latter collection won the 1987 Pulitzer Prize, making Dove the second African-American woman poet (after Gwendolyn Brooks in 1950) to receive the award. Many of her best poems, like "Daystar" from *Thomas and Beulah,* are lyrical and personal, employing plain statement and deriving drama from the immediacy of the moment. Appointed Poet Laureate of the United States for 1993 and 1994, Dove now teaches at the University of Virginia and, in addition to her poetry, has published a novel, a collection of short stories, and a verse drama.

Naomi Shihab Nye

Naomi Shihab Nye (1952–) was born in St. Louis, Missouri, to an American mother and a Palestinian father. She graduated from Trinity College in San Antonio, Texas, where she lives today with her husband and son. Nye has also lived in Jerusalem and has twice traveled to the Middle East and Asia for the United States Information Agency to promote international understanding through the arts. In addition to six volumes of poetry, Nye has published short stories and children's books, and she has edited several collections of poetry and prose.

Gary Soto

Gary Soto (1952–) was raised in a working-class family in Fresno, California. His interest in literature and writing developed while an undergraduate at Fresno State College, where he studied under Philip Levine. After graduation, he earned an M.F.A. at the University of California at Irvine. After residing for a time in Mexico, in 1977 Soto published his first book of poetry, *The Elements of San Joaquin,* to critical acclaim. Soto has since published several additional volumes of poetry and a prose memoir, *Living Up the Street* (1985), which won an American Book Award. He is also the editor of several poetry anthologies. His poetry is largely autobiographical, employing direct and plain diction with concrete images charged with his experience as a Mexican American.

Julia Alvarez

Although Julia Alvarez (1950–) was born in New York City, she spent her first decade living in the Dominican Republic. Her father brought the family to New York in 1960 after the fall of the Dominican dictator Trujillo. Alvarez has written three novels, a book of essays, and three collections of poetry. Throughout her work, she explores themes of identity and culture, as she poignantly portrays the immigrant experience in America. She divides her time between Vermont, where she teaches at Middlebury College, and the Dominican Republic, where she runs a coffee plantation with her husband. "Bilingual Sestina" is from *The Other Side/El Otro Lado* (1996).

Mary Jo Salter

Mary Jo Salter (1954–) was born in Grand Rapids, Michigan, the daughter of an advertising executive and an artist. Salter attended Harvard as an undergraduate and obtained an M.A. from Cambridge University. Afterwards, she lectured at Harvard and Mount Holyoke, serving a stint editing at *The Atlantic Monthly* and teaching English in Japan between appointments. Salter has written several volumes of poetry and *The Moon Comes Home* (1989), a children's book, in addition to editing *The Norton Anthology of Poetry* (1996). Her most recent book is *A Kiss in Space: Poems* (1999).

Cathy Song

Cathy Song (1955–) was born in Honolulu, Hawaii, to a Korean-American father and a Chinese-American mother. She received her undergraduate degree from Wellesley and a graduate degree from Boston University. Her first book of poems, *Picture Bride* (1983) includes "Lost Sister." Song's poetry fuses her knowledge of the visual arts and Western poetry with her experience as an Asian-American woman with a strong awareness of her East Asian heritage. In recent years she has lived and taught in Hawaii.

Li-Young Lee

Li-Young Lee (1957–) was born in Jakarta, Indonesia, of Chinese parents. In 1959, the Lee family fled Indonesia in the face of anti-Chinese sentiment. After five years of moving from country to country, the family settled in the United States. Educated at the University of Pittsburgh, the University of Arizona, and the State University of New York, Brockport, Lee has taught at several universities. In addition to his volumes of poetry, he has published a memoir, *The Winged Seed: A Remembrance* (1995). He lives in Chicago with his wife and two sons.

Rafael Campo

Born in Dover, New Jersey, to Cuban parents who fled Castro's regime, Rafael Campo (1964–) is a poet and a physician who currently practices medicine at Harvard Medical School and the Beth Israel Deaconess Medical Center in Boston. He has published three collections of poetry, including *Diva* (1999), a finalist for the National Book Critics Circle Award, and several books in prose, including *The Poetry of Healing* (1996). His identity as a gay male is thematized in much of his poetry.

Acknowledgments

Alvarez, "Bilingual Sestina": From *The Other Side/El Otro Lado*. Copyright © 1995 by Julia Alvarez. Published by Dutton, a division of Penguin USA. Reprinted by permission of Susan Bergholz Literary Services, New York. All rights reserved.

Ashbery, "Paradoxes and Oxymorons": From *Shadow Train*, by John Ashbery. Reprinted by permission of Georges Borchardt, Inc., for the author.

Atwood, "Siren Song": From *Selected Poems II: Poems Selected and New 1976–1986* by Margaret Atwood. Copyright © 1987 by Margaret Atwood. Reprinted by permission of Houghton Mifflin Company. All rights reserved.

Auden, "Musée des Beaux Arts": From *W. H. Auden: Collected Poems* by W. H. Auden. Used by permission of Random House, Inc.

Berryman, "Dream Song #4": From *The Dream Songs* by John Berryman. Copyright © 1969 by John Berryman. Copyright renewed 1997 by Kate Donahue Berryman. Reprinted by permission of Farrar, Straus and Giroux, LLC.

Bishop, "The Fish" and "Sestina": From *The Complete Poems 1927–1979* by Elizabeth Bishop. Copyright © 1979, 1983 by Alice Helen Methfessel. Reprinted by permission of Farrar, Straus and Giroux, LLC.

Brooks, "We Real Cool": From *Blacks* by Gwendolyn Brooks, © 1991, Third World Press, Chicago, IL. Reprinted by permission of the Estate of Gwendolyn Brooks.

Campo, "The Next Poem Could Be Your Last": VI. from "Song Before Dying": in *What the Body Told*, by Rafael Campo. Copyright © 1996 by Rafael Campo. Reprinted by permission of Georges Borchardt, Inc., for the author.

Clifton, "Homage to My Hips": Copyright © 1980, 1987 by Lucille Clifton. First appeared in *Two-Headed Woman*, published by the University of Massachusetts Press, 1980. Now appears in *Good Woman: Poems and a Memoir 1969–1980*, published by BOA Editions, Ltd. Reprinted by permission of Curtis Brown, Ltd.

Cullen, "Incident": From the book *Color* by Countee Cullen. Copyright © 1925 by Harper & Brothers; copyright renewed 1953 by Ida M. Cullen. Reprinted by permission of GRM Associates, Inc., as agents for the Estate of Ida M. Cullen.

Cummings, "in Just—" and "Buffalo Bill's": Copyright 1923, 1951, © 1991 by the Trustees for the E. E. Cummings Trust. Copyright © 1976 by George James Firmage. Used by permission of Liveright Publishing Corporation. "Anyone Lived in a Pretty How Town": Copyright 1940, © 1968, 1991 by the Trustees for the E. E. Cummings Trust, from *Complete Poems: 1904–1962 by E. E. Cummings*, edited by George J. Firmage. Used by permission of Liveright Publishing Corporation.

Dickinson, "After Great Pain, a Formal Feeling Comes," "The Soul Selects Her Own Society," and "I Heard a Fly Buzz—When I Died—": Reprinted by permission of the publishers and the Trustees of Amherst College from *The Poems of Emily Dickinson*, Thomas H. Johnson, ed., Cambridge, Mass.: The Belknap Press of Harvard University Press, Copyright © 1951, 1955, 1979 by the President and Fellows of Harvard College.

Dove, "Daystar": From *Thomas and Beulah*, Carnegie Mellon University Press, © 1986 by Rita Dove. Reprinted by permission of the author.

Eliot, "The Love Song of J. Alfred Prufrock" and "Preludes": From *Collected Poems 1909–1962* by T. S. Eliot, 1964. Reprinted by permission of Faber and Faber, Ltd.

Forché, "The Colonel": From *The Country between Us* by Carolyn Forché. Copyright © 1981 by Carolyn Forché. Originally appeared in *Women's International Resource Exchange.* Reprinted by permission of HarperCollins Publishers, Inc.

Frost, "After Apple-Picking," "Birches," and "Mending Wall": From *The Poetry of Robert Frost,* edited by Edward Connery Lathem. Copyright © 1969 by Henry Holt & Co., LLC. Reprinted by permission of Henry Holt and Company, LLC. "Stopping by Woods": From *The Poetry of Robert Frost,* edited by Edward Connery Lathem. Copyright 1951 by Robert Frost, © 1923 by Henry Holt & Co., LLC. Reprinted by permission of Henry Holt and Company, LLC.

Ginsberg, "A Supermarket in California": From *Collected Poems 1947–1980* by Allen Ginsberg. Copyright © 1955 by Allen Ginsberg. Copyright renewed. Reprinted by permission of HarperCollins Publishers, Inc.

Glück, "The Schoolchildren": From *The House on Marshland* in *The First Four Books of Poems* by Louise Glück. Copyright © 1968, 1971, 1972, 1973, 1974, 1975, 1976, 1977, 1978, 1979, 1980, 1985, 1995 by Louise Glück. Reprinted by permission of HarperCollins Publishers, Inc.

H. D., "Heat": From *Collected Poems, 1912–1944,* copyright © 1982 by the Estate of Hilda Doolittle. Reprinted by permission of New Directions Publishing Corp.

Harjo, "Eagle Poem": From *In Mad Love and War,* © 1990 by Joy Harjo, Wesleyan University Press, reprinted by permission of the author and University Press of New England.

Hayden, "Those Winter Sundays": Copyright © 1966 by Robert Hayden, from *Angle of Ascent: New and Selected Poems* by Robert Hayden. Used by permission of Liveright Publishing Corporation.

Heaney, "Digging": From *Opened Ground: Selected Poems 1966–1986* by Seamus Heaney. Copyright © 1998 by Seamus Heaney. Reprinted by permission of Farrar, Straus and Giroux, LLC and Faber and Faber, Ltd.

Hughes, "Harlem (Dream Deferred)," "The Negro Speaks of Rivers," and "Mother to Son": From *The Collected Poems of Langston Hughes* by Langston Hughes, copyright © 1994 by the Estate of Langston Hughes. Used by permission of Alfred A. Knopf, a division of Random House, Inc.

Jarrell, "The Death of the Ball Turret Gunner": From *The Complete Poems* by Randall Jarrell. Copyright © 1969, renewed 1997 by Mary von S. Jarrell. Reprinted by permission of Farrar, Straus and Giroux, LLC.

Komunyakaa, "Facing It": From *Dien Cai Dau,* © 1988 by Yusef Komunyakaa, Wesleyan University Press, reprinted by permission of University Press of New England.

Larkin, "Aubade": From *Collected Poems* by Philip Larkin. Copyright © 1988, 1989 by the Estate of Philip Larkin. Reprinted by permission of Farrar, Straus and Giroux, LLC and Faber and Faber, Ltd.

Lee, "Eating Together": Reprinted from *Rose: Poems* by Li-Young Lee, with the permission of BOA Editions, Ltd.

Lowell, "For the Union Dead": From *For the Union Dead* by Robert Lowell. Copyright © 1959 by Robert Lowell. Copyright renewed © 1987 by Harriet Lowell, Caroline Lowell, and Sheridan Lowell. Reprinted by permission of Farrar, Straus and Giroux, LLC.

MacLeish, "Ars Poetica": From *Collected Poems 1917–1982* by Archibald Macleish. Copyright © 1985 by The Estate of Archibald Macleish. Reprinted by permission of Houghton Mifflin Company. All rights reserved.

Millay, "What Lips My Lips Have Kissed, and Where, and Why": From *Collected Poems,* HarperCollins. Copyright © 1923, 1951 by Edna St. Vincent Millay and Norma Millay Ellis. All rights reserved. Reprinted by permission of Elizabeth Barnett, literary executor.

Moore, "A Grave" and "Poetry": Reprinted with the permission of Scribner, a Division of Simon & Schuster, from *The Collected Poems of Marianne Moore.* Copyright 1935 by Marianne Moore; copyright renewed © 1963 by Marianne Moore and T. S. Eliot.

Nims, "Love Poem": From *Selected Poems* by John Frederick Nims. Reprinted by permission of the University of Chicago Press.

Nye, "The Traveling Onion": Reprinted by permission of the author, Naomi Shihab Nye, 2000.

Olds, "The One Girl at the Boys' Party": From *The Dead and the Living* by Sharon Olds, copyright © 1987 by Sharon Olds. Used by permission of Alfred A. Knopf, a division of Random House, Inc.

Oliver, "The Storm": From *Winter Hours* by Mary Oliver. Copyright © 1999 by Mary Oliver. Reprinted by permission of Houghton Mifflin Co. All rights reserved.

Parker, "Résumé": Copyright 1926, 1928, renewed 1954, © 1956 by Dorothy Parker, from *The Portable Dorothy Parker* by Dorothy Parker. Used by permission of Viking Penguin, a division of Penguin Putnam, Inc.

Pastan, "Ethics": From *Waiting for My Life*, by Linda Pastan. Copyright © 1981 by Linda Pastan. Used by permission of W. W. Norton & Company, Inc.

Piercy, "Barbie Doll": From *Circles on the Water* by Marge Piercy, copyright © 1982 by Marge Piercy. Used by permission of Alfred A. Knopf, a division of Random House, Inc.

Plath, "Metaphors": From *Crossing the Water* by Sylvia Plath. Copyright © 1960 by Ted Hughes. Copyright renewed. Reprinted by permission of HarperCollins Publishers, Inc. and Faber and Faber, Ltd. "Daddy": From *Ariel* by Sylvia Plath. Copyright © 1963 by Ted Hughes. Copyright renewed. Reprinted by permission of HarperCollins Publishers, Inc. and Faber and Faber, Ltd.

Pound, "In a Station of the Metro" and "The River-Merchant's Wife: A Letter": From *Personae*, copyright © 1926 by Ezra Pound. Reprinted by permission of New Directions Publishing Corp.

Ransom, "Bells for John Whiteside's Daughter": Copyright 1924 by Alfred A. Knopf, Inc. and renewed 1952 by John Crowe Ransom. From *Selected Poems* by John Crowe Ransom. Reprinted by permission of the publisher.

Roethke, "My Papa's Waltz": From *Collected Poems* of Theodore Roethke by Theodore Roethke, copyright 1966. Used by permission of Doubleday, a division of Random House, Inc.

Salter, "Boulevard du Montparnasse": From *Sunday Skaters* by Mary Jo Salter. Copyright © 1994 by Mary Jo Salter. Reprinted by permission of Alfred A. Knopf, Inc.

Sandburg, "Fog" and "A Fence": From *Chicago Poems* by Carl Sandburg, copyright 1916 by Holt, Rinehart and Winston and renewed 1944 by Carl Sandburg, reprinted by permission of Harcourt, Inc.

Sexton, "Cinderella": From *Transformations*. Copyright © 1971 by Anne Sexton. Reprinted by permission of Houghton Mifflin Co. All rights reserved.

Silko, "Prayer to the Pacific": From *Storyteller* by Leslie Marmon Silko. Copyright © 1981 by Leslie Marmon Silko. Reprinted by permission of the Wylie Agency, Inc.

Snyder, "A Walk": From *The Back Country*, copyright © 1968 by Gary Snyder. Reprinted by permission of New Directions Publishing Corp.

Song, "Lost Sister": From *Picture Bride* by Cathy Song. Copyright © 1983 by Cathy Song. Reprinted by permission of Yale University Press.

Soto, "Oranges": From *New and Selected Poems* by Gary Soto. Published by Chronicle Books, San Francsico. Reprinted by permission.

Stafford, "Traveling through the Dark": From *The Way It Is*, copyright 1962, 1988 by the Estate of William Stafford. Reprinted with the permission of Graywolf Press, Saint Paul, Minnesota.

Steele, "An Aubade": Reprinted by permission of the University of Arkansas Press. Copyright 1986 by Timothy Steele.

Stevens, "The Snow Man," "Emperor of Ice-Cream," and "13 Ways of Looking at a Blackbird": From *The Collected Poems of Wallace Stevens* by Wallace Stevens, copyright 1954 by Wallace Stevens. Used by permission of Alfred A. Knopf, a division of Random House, Inc.

Strand, "The Tunnel": From *Selected Poems* by Mark Strand, copyright © 1979, 1980 by Mark Strand. Used by permission of Alfred A. Knopf, a division of Random House, Inc.

Thomas, "Fern Hill" and **"Do Not Go Gentle into That Good Night":** From *The Poems of Dylan Thomas*, copyright © 1952 by Dylan Thomas. Reprinted by permission of New Directions Publishing Corp. and David Higham.

Toomer, "Song of the Son" and **"Reapers":** From *Cane* by Jean Toomer. Copyright 1923 by Boni & Liveright, renewed 1951 by Jean Toomer. Used by permission of Liveright Publishing Corporation.

Wilbur, "Love Calls Us to the Things of This World": From *Things of This World* by Richard Wilbur, copyright 1956 and renewed 1984 by Richard Wilbur, reprinted by permission of Harcourt, Inc.

Williams, "To Waken an Old Lady," "This Is Just to Say," and **"The Red Wheelbarrow":** From *Collected Poems, 1909–1939: Volume I,* copyright © 1938 by New Directions Publishing Corp. Reprinted by permission of New Directions Publishing Corp.

Wright, "A Blessing": From *Above the River: The Complete Poems,* © 1990 by Anne Wright, Wesleyan University Press, reprinted by permission of University Press of New England.

Yeats, "Sailing to Byzantium": Reprinted with the permission of Scribner, a division of Simon & Schuster, from *The Collected Poems of W. B. Yeats,* Revised Second Edition, edited by Richard Finneran. Copyright 1928 by Macmillan Publishing Company; copyright renewed © 1956 by Georgie Yeats.

Text

Context

Western Wind [ca. 1500]	**1500**	Da Vinci, *Mona Lisa* (1503)
		Michelangelo, *David* (ca. 1504);
		Sistine Chapel (1508–12)
		Luther's 95 Theses introduce
		Reformation in Europe (1517)

	1550	Reign of Elizabeth I (1558–1603);
		Breughel, *Landscape with the Fall of*
		Icarus (c. 1558)
		Raleigh's expedition to Virginia
		(1584)
		Defeat of Spanish Armada by
Marlowe (1564–1593): *The*		England (1588)
Passionate Shepherd to His Love		Globe Theatre built in London
(1599)		(1599)

Raleigh (1552–1618): *The Nymph's*   **1600**   Bodleian Library, Oxford
Reply (1600)   University, opens (1602)
Jonson (1573?–1637): *On My First*   James I succeeds Elizabeth (1603)
Son [1603]; *To Celia* (1616)   Galileo constructs astronomical
Shakespeare (1564–1616): *Sonnets*   telescope (1608)
(1609)
Donne (1572–1631): *Death Be Not*
Proud [ca. 1610]; *A Valediction:*
Forbidding Mourning [1611]; *Song*
(1633)
Campion (1567–1620): *There Is a*
Garden in Her Face (1617)
Drayton (1563–1631): *Since There's*   Thirty Years' War (1618–1648)
No Help (1619)   Pilgrims sail for America (1620)
Herbert (1593–1633): *Easter Wings*
(1633)
Herrick (1591–1674): *To the Virgins,*   Parliament closes British theaters;
To Make Much of Time (1648)   English Civil War (1642–9)
Lovelace (1618–1658): *To Lucasta,*
on Going to the Wars (1649)

Milton (1608–1674): *When I*   **1650**   Cromwell's Protectorate (1653–8)
Consider How My Light Is Spent   Restoration of Charles II (1660)
[1655?]   Reign of Louis XIV, the "Sun King"
Bradstreet (1612?–1672): *The*   (1661–1715)
Author to Her Book (1678); *To My*   Rembrandt, *Return of the Prodigal*
Dear and Loving Husband (1678)   *Son* (1668–9)
Marvell (1621–1678): *To His Coy*   Newton's laws of gravity (1687)
Mistress (1681)   William and Mary succeed James II
                          (Glorious Revolution: 1688)

Text

Context

Text		Context
Swift (1667–1745): *A Description of the Morning;* Pope (1688–1744): *An Essay on Criticism* (1711); *Epigram* (1738)	**1700**	Peter the Great begins Westernization of Russia (ca. 1701) Baroque music flourishes (Bach and Handel, ca. 1724)
Wheatley (1753?–1784): *To the University of Cambridge* (1773) Blake (1757–1827): *The Tyger* (1794); *The Sick Rose* (1794); *London* (1794) Coleridge (1772–1834): *Kubla Khan* [1797–98]	**1750**	Catherine the Great of Russia begins reign (1762) *Sturm und Drang* ("Storm and Stress") movement in Germany (1767–87) Watt patents steam engine (1769) American Revolution (1775–1781); Declaration of Independence (1776) Mozart, *Don Giovanni* (1787) French Revolution begins (1789)
Wordsworth (1770–1850): *Lines Composed a Few Miles above Tintern Abbey* (1798); *Composed upon Westminster Bridge* (1807); *The World Is Too Much with Us* (1807) Byron (1788–1824): *When We Two Parted* (1813); *She Walks in Beauty* (1814) Shelley (1792–1822): *Ozymandias* (1818); *Ode to the West Wind* (1820) Keats (1795–1821): *When I Have Fears That I May Cease to Be* [1818]; *To Autumn* (1820); *Ode on a Grecian Urn* (1820) Poe (1809–1849): *To Helen* (1831); *The Raven* (1845) Tennyson (1809–1892): *Ulysses* [1833]; *Tears, Idle Tears* (1847) R. Browning (1812–1889): *My Last Duchess* (1842) E. Browning (1806–1861): *How Do I Love Thee? Let Me Count the Ways* (1850)	**1800**	Beginnings of English Romanticism (ca. 1800); Napoleon becomes Emperor of France (1804) Beethoven, *Fifth Symphony* (1810) Napoleon defeated at Waterloo (1815) Berlioz, *Symphonie Fantastique* (1830) American Transcendentalists meet in Boston and Concord (1836) Queen Victoria accedes to English throne (1837) Samuel Morse invents the telegraph (1844) Seneca Falls Convention for Women's Rights (1848)
Whitman (1819–1892): *Song of Myself, 6* (1855); *When I Heard the Learn'd Astronomer* (1865); *Cavalry Crossing a Ford* [1865]; *A Noiseless Patient Spider* [1876]	**1850**	*Dredd Scott* Supreme Court decision denies citizenship to African Americans (1857) Transatlantic cable laid (1858)

Text	Context
Dickinson (1830–1886): *Wild Nights—Wild Nights!* [ca. 1861]; *The Soul Selects Her Own Society* [ca. 1862]; *I Heard a Fly Buzz—When I Died* [ca. 1862]; *After Great Pain, a Formal Feeling Comes* [1862] Rossetti (1830–1894): *Uphill* (1862) Arnold (1822–1888): *Dover Beach* (1867)	**1850** **(cont.)** U.S. Civil War (1861–5); Lincoln assassinated (1865)
Hopkins (1844–1889): *God's Grandeur* [1877]; *Pied Beauty* [1877] Yeats (1865–1939): *The Lake Isle of Innisfree* (1892); *When You Are Old* (1893); *The Second Coming* (1921); *Sailing to Byzantium* (1927) Housman (1859–1936): *To an Athlete Dying Young* (1896); *Loveliest of Trees, the Cherry Now* (1896) Dunbar (1872–1906): *We Wear the Mask* (1896)	Telephone patented; Wagner's Festspielhaus opened (1876) Edison invents phonograph (1877) and light bulb (1879) Eiffel Tower built for the 1889 Paris World's Fair (1887) Van Gogh, *Starry Night* (1889) X-rays discovered (1895) Radium discovered (1898)
Robinson (1869–1935): *Richard Cory* (1897); *Mr. Flood's Party* (1921) Hardy (1840–1928): *Neutral Tones* (1898); *The Man He Killed* (1909) Frost (1874–1963): *Mending Wall* (1914); *After Apple-Picking* (1914); *Birches* (1916); *Stopping by Woods on a Snowy Evening* (1923) Pound (1885–1972): *The River-Merchant's Wife: A Letter* (1915); *In a Station of the Metro* (1916) Lowell (1874–1925): *Patterns;* H. D. (1886–1961): *Heat;* Sandburg (1878–1967): *Fog; A Fence* (1916) Eliot (1888–1965): *The Love Song of J. Alfred Prufrock* (1917); *Preludes* (1917) Stevens (1879–1955): *13 Ways of Looking at a Blackbird* (1917); *The Snow Man* (1921); *Emperor of Ice-Cream* (1922) Williams (1883–1963): *To Waken an Old Lady* (1920); *The Red Wheelbarrow* (1923); *This Is Just to Say* (1934)	**1900** Marconi's first transatlantic radiotelegraph message (1901) Wright brothers make successful airplane flight (1903) Einstein's theory of relativity (1905) Picasso, *Les Demoiselles d'Avignon* (1907) NAACP founded in New York (1909) W. C. Handy publishes "Memphis Blues" to great acclaim; Republic of China replaces Manchu dynasty (1912) Stravinsky, *The Rites of Spring* (1913) World War I (1914–8) Russian Revolution; U.S. enters World War I (1917) End of WW I ushers in worldwide influenza epidemic, which kills 22 million; major race riots in U.S. (1918) Prohibition ratified in U.S. (1919)

Text

Context

Text	Context
Cummings (1894–1962): *Buffalo Bill's* (1920); *in Just-* (1923); *anyone lived in a pretty how town* (1940)	**1900** (cont.) Women's suffrage in U.S. (1920)
Millay (1892–1950): *First Fig* (1920); *What Lips My Lips Have Kissed, and Where, and Why* (1923)	
Owen (1893–1918): *Dulce et Decorum Est* (1920)	Harlem Renaissance flourishes
McKay (1889–1948): *America* (1921)	(1920s)
Hughes (1902–1967): *The Negro Speaks of Rivers* (1921); *Mother to Son* (1922); *Harlem* (1951)	
Wylie (1885–1928): *Wild Peaches;*	Schoenberg's twelve-tone music (1926)
Moore (1887–1972): *A Grave; Poetry* (1921)	*The Jazz Singer;* Lindbergh crosses Atlantic (1927)
Toomer (1894–1967): *Song of the Son* (1922); *Reapers* (1923)	Stock market crash (1929) ushers in Great Depression in the U.S.
Ransom (1888–1974): *Bells for John Whiteside's Daughter;* Cullen (1903–1946): *Incident* (1924)	FDR's "New Deal": introduces social security, welfare, and unemployment insurance (1932)
Parker (1893–1967): *Résumé;* MacLeish (1892–1982): *Ars Poetica* (1926)	Nazis gain control of Germany (1933)
Auden (1907–1973): *Musée des Beaux Arts* (1940)	Jesse Owens wins 4 gold medals in track at the Olympics in Berlin (1935)
Jarrell (1914–1965): *The Death of the Ball Turret Gunner* (1945)	First television broadcast (1936) Spanish Civil War (1936–39)
Thomas (1914–1953): *Fern Hill* (1946); *Do Not Go Gentle into That Good Night* (1952)	Joe Lewis becomes heavyweight champion of the world (1937) World War II (1939–45)
Bishop (1911–1979): *The Fish* (1946); *Sestina* (1965)	Japan bombs Pearl Harbor (1941) U.S. drops atomic bomb on Japan;
Nims (1913–1999): *Love Poem* (1947)	U.N. formed (1945) Nuremberg trials (1946)
Roethke (1908–1963): *My Papa's Waltz* (1948)	India achieves independence (1947) Germany divided; People's Republic of China established (1949)
Ginsberg (1926–1997): *A Supermarket in California* (1955)	**1950** Korean War (1950–53) DNA discovered (1953)
Wilbur (1921–): *Love Calls Us to the Things of This World* (1956)	*Brown v. Board of Education;* McCarthy-Army hearings (1954)
Lowell (1917–1977): *For the Union Dead* (1959)	Rosa Parks arrested in Montgomery for refusing to give
Plath (1932–1963): *Metaphors* (1960); *Daddy* (1965)	her seat to a white man on a bus; ignites Civil Rights Movement (1955)

Text	Context
Brooks (1917–2000): *We Real Cool* (1960)	**1950** (cont.) Russia crushes revolt in Hungary (1956)
Wright (1927–1980): *A Blessing* (1961)	Cuban Revolution (1959)
Hayden (1913–1980): *Those Winter Sundays;* Stafford (1914–1993): *Traveling through the Dark* (1962)	Berlin Wall erected (1961)
Berryman (1914–1972): *Dream Song #4* (1964)	Cuban Missile crisis (1962)
Heaney (1939–): *Digging* (1966)	Martin Luther King, Jr. delivers "I Have a Dream"; Kennedy assassinated (1963)
Strand (1934–): *The Tunnel;* Snyder (1930–): *A Walk* (1968)	U.S. enters Vietnam War; Malcolm X assassinated; Watts riots (Los Angeles) (1965)
Piercy (1936–): *Barbie Doll* (1969)	Mao Zedong's Cultural Revolution begins (1966)
Sexton (1928–1974): *Cinderella* (1970)	King assassinated (1968)
Glück (1943–): *The School Children* (1971)	American astronauts land on the moon (1969)
Atwood (1939–): *Siren Song* (1974)	Watergate burglary (1972)
Larkin (1922–1985): *Aubade* (1977)	
Forché (1950–): *The Colonel* (1978)	
Pastan (1932–): *Ethics* (1980)	Islamic revolution in Iran (1979)
Ashbery (1927–): *Paradoxes and Oxymorons;* Leslie Marmon Silko (1948–): *Prayer to the Pacific* (1981)	
Olds (1942–): *The One Girl at the Boys' Party;* Song (1955–): *Lost Sister* (1983)	
Lee (1957–): *Eating Together* (1985)	
Steele (1948–): *An Aubade;* Dove (1952–): *Daystar;* Nye (1952–): *The Traveling Onion* (1986)	
Komunyakaa (1947–): *Facing It* (1988)	
Harjo (1951–): *Eagle Poem* (1990)	Berlin Wall is demolished; Eastern Europe democratized (1989)
Clifton (1936–): *Homage to My Hips* (1991)	Soviet Union dissolves (1991)
Salter (1954–): *Boulevard du Montparnasse* (1994)	NAFTA takes effect (1994)
Alvarez (1950–): *Bilingual Sestina;* Soto (1952–): *Oranges* (1995)	
Campo (1964–): *The Next Poem Could Be Your Last* (1996)	
Oliver (1935–): *The Storm* (1999)	
	2000 George W. Bush elected president (2000)

Index